DALVEY 7: HOUSES BY 7 SINGAPORE ARCHITECTS

Publishers of Architecture, Art, and Design
Gordon Goff: Publisher

www.oroeditions.com
info@oroeditions.com

Published by ORO Editions

Copyright © K2LD Architects 2020
Text and Images © K2LD Architects 2020

All rights reserved. No part of this book may be reproduced, stored in a retrieval system, or transmitted in any form or by any means, including electronic, mechanical, photocopying of microfilming, recording, or otherwise (except that copying permitted by Sections 107 and 108 of the U.S. Copyright Law and except by reviewers for the public press) without written permission from the publisher.

You must not circulate this book in any other binding or cover and you must impose this same condition on any acquirer.

Graphic Design: Duet Design, Singapore
Text: Erwin Viray, Ko Shiou Hee and Patrick Bingham-Hall
ORO Project Coordinator: Kirby Anderson

10 9 8 7 6 5 4 3 2 1 First Edition

Library of Congress data available upon request.
World Rights: Available

ISBN: 978-1-943532-93-3

Color Separations and Printing: ORO Group Ltd.
Printed in China.

International Distribution: www.oroeditions.com/distribution

ORO Editions makes a continuous effort to minimise the overall carbon footprint of its publications. As part of this goal, ORO Editions, in association with Global ReLeaf, arranges to plant trees to replace those used in the manufacturing of the paper produced for its books. Global ReLeaf is an international campaign run by American Forests, one of the world's oldest nonprofit conservation organizations. Global ReLeaf is American Forests' education and action program that helps individuals, organizations, agencies, and corporations improve the local and global environment by planting and caring for trees.

DALVEY 7: HOUSES BY 7 SINGAPORE ARCHITECTS

FOREWORD

Dalvey 7 is a delightful book, bringing seven architects—Wallflower, Guz Architects, AR43, Aamer Architects, K2LD, ipli, CSYA—to imagine a possible way of creating architecture.

K2LD brought everyone together, believing that collaboration is paramount to push forward the profession and practice of architecture, and worked with the clients to select the other collaborating architects.

A house is a fertile field of exploration for an architect for innovations in space, construction, materials, and quality of life within its appropriate space. In *Dalvey 7*, we see not only an expression of the architect but a conversation and collaboration. Each architect has administered care to orient a house in relation to its neighbours, to appreciate a view, to integrate trees, to consider wind flow, to use existing structures to provide a new life and a memory. Each house expresses emotion, a life, while mindful of neighbours.

In hearing conversations between architects, I recalled the Renga (連歌)—a genre of Japanese collaborative poetry written by more than one author working together. It consists of at least two ku (句) or stanzas. The opening stanza called the hokku (発句), became the basis for the modern haiku form of poetry. In basic Renga, the first line is five syllables and the second line is seven syllables; the third line consists of five syllables and then the collaborative poet finishes the stanza by adding two more lines which are seven syllables in length. The participants compose line with 5-7-5-7-7 syllables with relevant key words current to the time and the context.

For *Dalvey 7*, it is a pleasure contributing a foreword for the different architectural voices, hearing them harmonise together to recite a poem illustrating a good environment, pleasing to the residents and the community.

Erwin Viray

TABLE OF CONTENTS

010
Dalvey 7

018
Collaborative Housing:
An Urban Anomaly

026
The Dalvey Estate:
Planning for Harmony

032
The Seven Villas:
Expression and Deference

PLOT
01
034
See Through House
by Wallflower Architects

02
058
Sail House
by Guz Architects

03
082
Tembusu House
by AR43 Architects

04
106
Gallery House
by Aamer Architects

PLOT
05
130
Orizuru House
by K2LD Architects

06
154
Old Dalvey
by ipli Architects

07
178
Long House
by CSYA Architects

202-207
The Seven Architects, Project Data, Credits

DALVEY SEVEN

Ko Shiou Hee

```
1 point is
   just a
   point.

   2 points
              form a line _____

      3 points compose
                s
             p     a
             c         e,

  and also begins
        to prove

                  a principle

        and

              p    a   tte    r n.
```

GIVING AND RECEIVING

The Dalvey Seven estate is the third collaborative architecture project spearheaded by K2LD. In 2004, K2LD led a group of five architects into China for: Huafa Ecovilla project in Zhongshan, Guangdong. This was followed by another successful collaboration in 2009, where K2LD invited five architects to each design one good-class-bungalow in the Lien Villa Collective at Holland Park, with K2LD responsible for designing the sixth house and the masterplan.

When K2LD was commissioned in 2015 by the Dalvey Estate family to select and lead a group of architects on a real estate development project comprised of seven houses, it was a confirmation and affirmation to me that my principle of sharing and collaboration does bear fruit. In giving, one receives.

PROFOUND INFLUENCES

I was deeply influenced by Issey Miyake in my formative years of architectural study. I chanced upon his book, *East Meets West*, and two things he wrote have stayed very close to my heart:

> I am always curious, not a passive kind of curiosity dependent upon information received but an active one that compels one to seek and ascertain the truth for oneself. I make it a point to hunt down uncertainties, to attack conventionalism… the obvious; and I have no precise method. With the result that our collaborations are never the same.
>
> My creation is never complete until the wearer wears it.
> – Issey Miyake

The first quote has become my modus operandi in my life journey and my entire work ethos. It reminds me never to be complacent, and to stay humble and curious.

The second quote reminds me not to be a "prima donna" architect. As an architect, I always seek to share my ideas with my colleagues, my clients, my friends, my students and my peers. I truly believe that architecture is not complete until the occupants are happy in it. These values that I hold dear have opened doors and placed me in positions where I can put these beliefs into practice.

While collaborative architecture projects are relatively rare in general, there have been some seminal projects that lit the path for me. Arata Isozaki's (Pritzker Prize winner 2019) Nexus I and Nexus II in Fukuoka, and another collective housing project in Kitagata, Gifu, wherein four female

DALVEY SEVEN

Nexus World, Fukuoka, Japan

Kitagata, Gifu, Japan

Commune by the Great Wall, China

architects had a very profound influence on me during my two-year stint in Japan. Isozaki parcelled out the housing plots and invited international up-and-coming architects (including Rem Koolhaas, Christian Portzamparc, Elizabeth Diller + Scorfidio, SAANA, to name a few) to collaborate on the design of the various parcels. This resulted in a unique typological innovation. More recently, the Commune by the Great Wall developed by SOHO was a similar endeavour to foster a collaborative process for a superior outcome.

GAME THEORY: WIN-WIN

Today, in the climate of spiritual self-centeredness, inward-turning and increased protectionism as manifested by Brexit, President Donald Trump's "America First" stance, the US-China trade war and the irresponsible burning of the Amazon forest in Brazil, I am reminded of the ground-breaking Game Theory by John Nash (Nobel Prize, 2000) and John von Neumann that helped to bring an end to the Cold War.

This mathematically proven model convinced the United States government to re-assess the risks and benefits of the Cold War, and to formulate on a win-win scenario to end the escalating tensions between different interest groups. History has shown that if everyone is for himself to maximise one's own profit, the world that we live in would be in a sad state.

Inspired by the Game Theory, I convinced my clients to adopt this sharing strategy in both the Lien Collective and the Dalvey Seven developments. The architects selected to participate must all adhere to the rules of the game, and work on the same fees and briefs. We all have to consider one another's placements and planning to maximise the benefit for all parties as a whole, and ultimately benefit the client. As architects, we have been educated to work with social, economic, and environmental sensitivity. Yet, the world that we operate in is driven by developers and stakeholders who prioritise maximizing their gains through development strategies, leaving architects scant space to be true to our profession. It is therefore even more pressing for architects to seize upon the collaborative spirit in this increasingly distortive and egocentric world.

DIVERSE SINGAPORE

I am grateful to be working in Singapore as an architect. Ours is a multicultural, multi-ethnic society that we often take for granted. If we would simply open our eyes and look around, we would realise that our colleagues in the profession are from all over the world. In the Dalvey Seven group, we have Guz Wilkinson from England and Aamer Taher whose mixed parentage is traced back partly to Pakistan.

In 2004, I led a group of "Singaporean" architects to work on the Ecovilla in Zhongshan, China for the Chinese developer Huafa. The group

DALVEY SEVEN

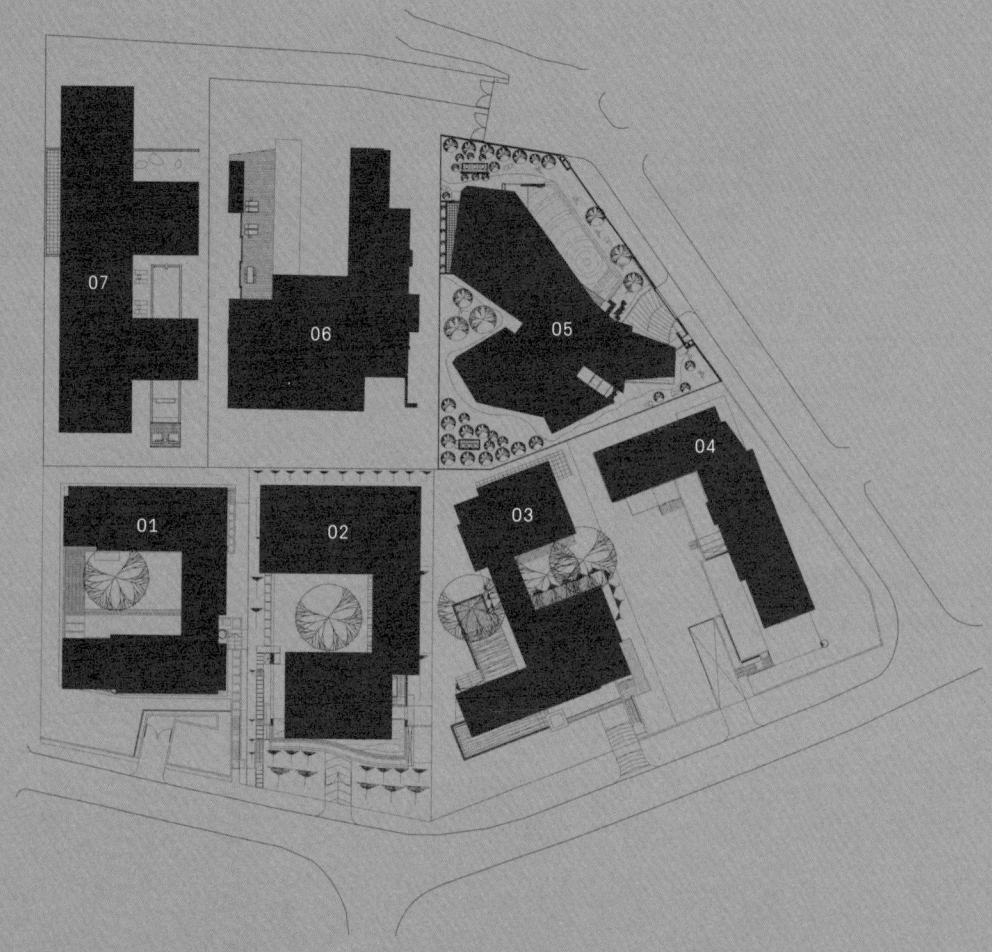

Master plan diagram of Dalvey Estate

included Ernesto Bedmar, originally from Argentina, Guz Wilkinson, and Aamer Taher, as well as native Singaporeans like myself (K2LD), Teh Joo Heng and Alvin Khor (AKDA). Our Chinese developer client was surprised to see our cosmopolitan group, but quickly came to realise that the unique characteristic of Singapore is its people from multi-national backgrounds who come to work here, love this country, and eventually make it their home.

It was this unique openness, established at the founding of Singapore, that attracted talent from all over the world. Yet, today, policies have been enacted to limit the influx of foreign talent for fear of competition. I wish to argue that it is exactly this competitive spirit, this diversity, that we need. It will train us to better survive the increasing threats and challenges from the world.

EMBRACE COMPETITION

Being aware of existential threats should compel us to embrace competition and to sharpen our edge rather than recede into protectionism. I applied the spirit of openness in sharing both the Lien Collective and Dalvey Seven projects where I truly believe, the challenges and "benign threat" from one's peers would compel us to perform better, and thus achieve a superior outcome than if we were to act alone.

Dalvey Seven is not a coincidence. I believe we have once again proven the Game Theory true. I hope the successes of these development projects will further encourage those of us in the architecture profession to share and collaborate. It is also an impetus to devise means to achieve that condition. I would like to see more, and different forms of joint ventures, of various scales: big firm-small firm; local firm-foreign firm; developer-architect ventures; design-built, etc. We can and must all aim to be better winners together.

DALVEY SEVEN

Group presentation to the client in 2016.

Assembled model of Dalvey 7 during 2016 client presentation at the Old Dalvey House.

COLLABORATIVE HOUSING: AN URBAN ANOMALY

Patrick Bingham-Hall

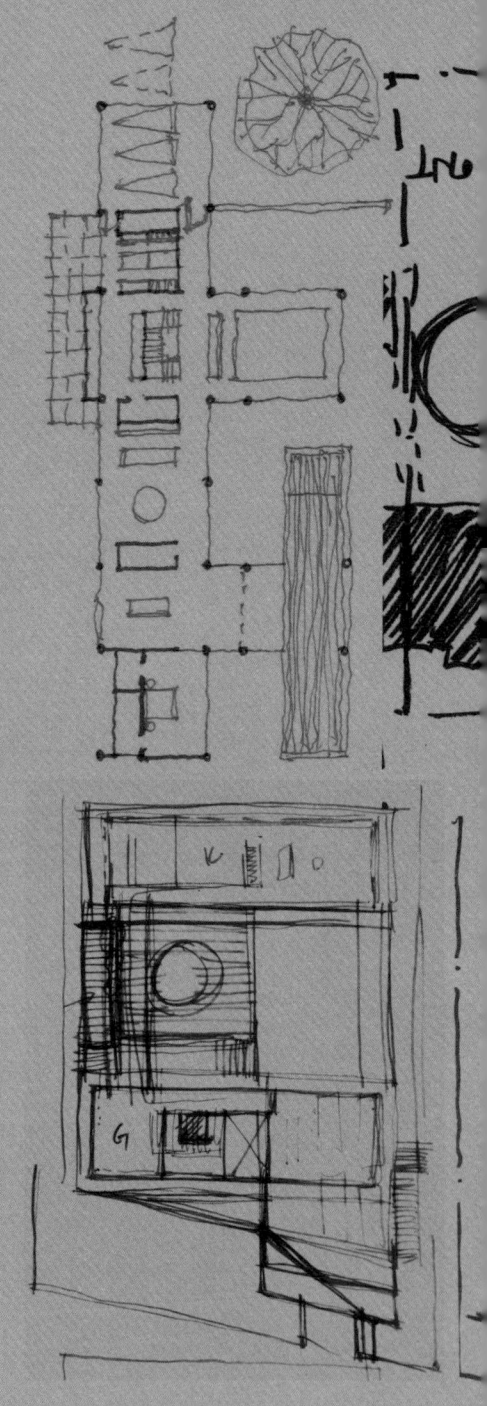

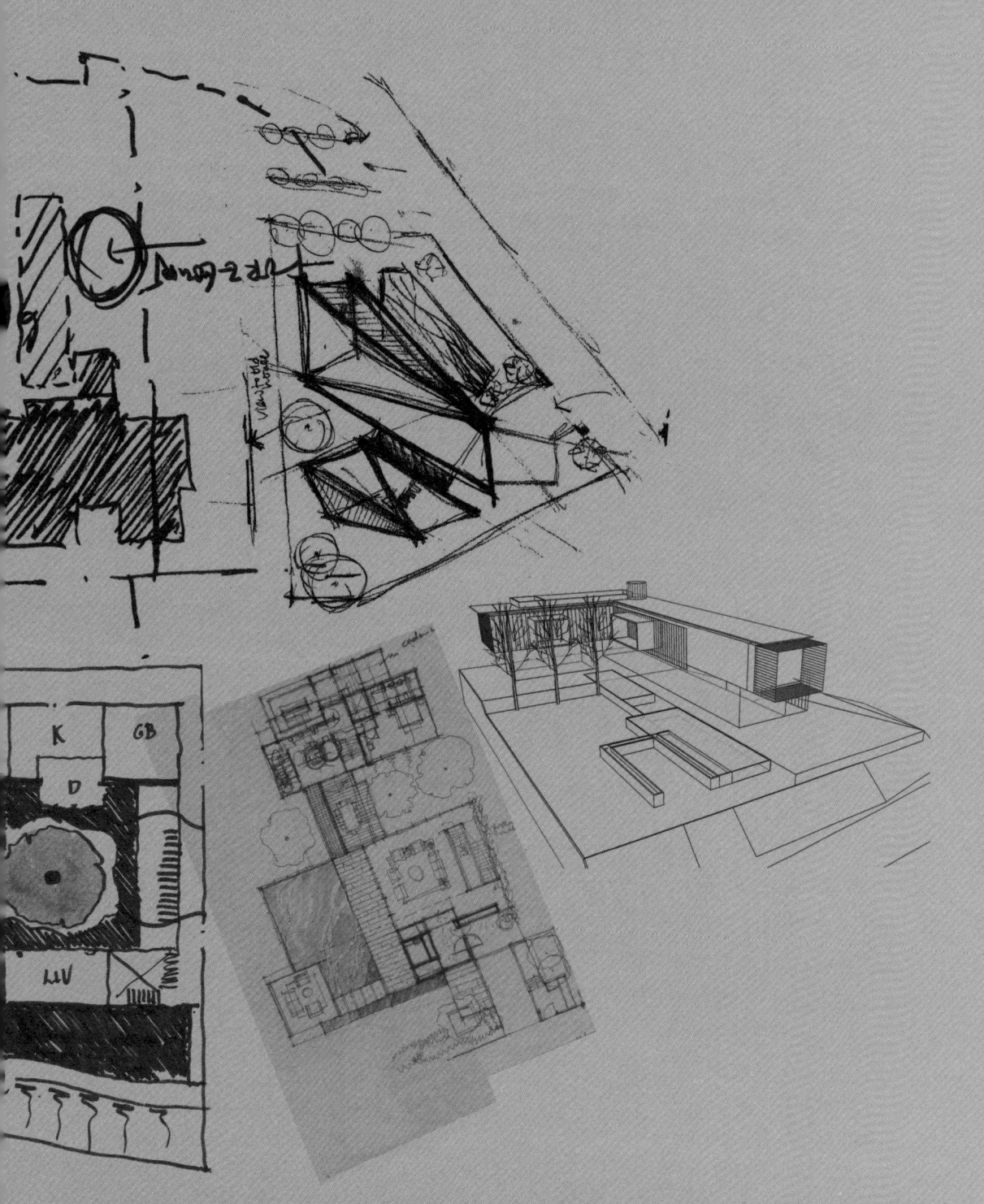

COLLABORATIVE HOUSING: AN URBAN ANOMALY

The first thing that strikes you when writing about collaborative urban housing is how rarely it has been done. An architect's desire for creative autonomy is infamous, even the nicest of architects harbours a self-belief that has long been deemed essential for their trade, and the notion of sharing, of engaging in mutual consultation with a collection of their peers is, to an architect, innately perplexing.

When working on a grand scale, say for the Olympic Games or urban renewal mega-schemes, architectural practices are obliged to acknowledge a context created by the adjacency of other new buildings, but at the level of the reasonably well-remunerated 'boutique' project, individual self-resource remains the architect's default setting. Which is an anomalous position to take with a form of creativity that would never be described as a mere profession by its younger and more zealous practitioners. Architecture has always been regarded as the 'mother of the arts' and its exponents, no matter what the scale or function of a commission, cannot help but assume exclusive pride in their greater calling. All well and good, Ayn Rand wrote *The Fountainhead* in honour of visionary architects in shining armour, but one must occasionally observe that ingrained self-regard has precluded many architects from obtaining the pleasures, not to mention the benefits that accrue from the essentially collaborative nature of other art forms. Architects don't exhibit their final works in public galleries, they don't play in orchestras, and they might be missing out on something.

As already observed, large practices or branded starchitects are accustomed to exhibiting their works at a grand civic scale alongside one another, but the extent to which they engage in consultation with each other is—judging by the results—minimal, to say the least. At the Marina Bay development for example, the architects designed monumental self-referential artefacts according to an overall masterplan which actively

FIG. 1 The Commune by the Great Wall in Beijing, China

encouraged creative indulgence instead of a cohesive urban morphology. Iconic city-scale image making is not achieved by fraternal deference, well not since Baron Hausmann and Napoleon III. One might have thought that at the level of the bespoke private house, architects might have welcomed the possibility of collaboration, of being invited to participate in a curated exhibit, to show off their designs in a 'sculpture garden for houses'. But it would appear not, even though it would be a good public relations exercise for architecture in general, and for individual architects, who might benefit from the demonstration of an inclusive temperament now appropriate for cheek-by-jowl suburban living. One celebrated Asian project, The Commune by the Great Wall in China (1997-2002), was conceptualised as a 'sculpture garden for houses' (FIG. 1), but as many of the architects were already very well-known, the location was rural and touristic, and the houses were set far apart, the implications and problem-resolutions for any urban equivalent were negligible.

Apart from creative intransigence, one elemental reason for the dearth of houses designed by collectives is a logistical difficulty, as perceived by the site owner or property developer, who would prefer a one-size-fits-all program of design and construction. Townhouse and condominium developments in Singapore have favoured a homogenous approach to design and landscape, and the results have mostly been quite delightful. Repetition of form and materials are intrinsic to one's expectation of such

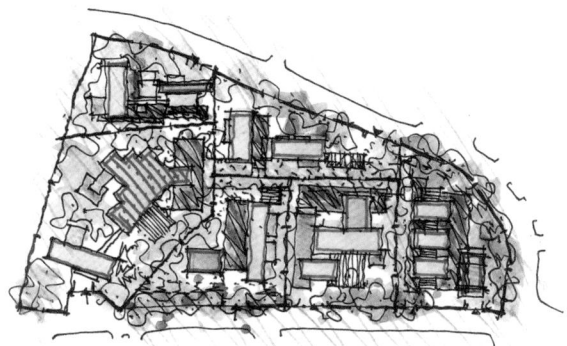

FIG. 2 A sketch of the Lien Villas Collective

developments, and a divergence from such harmony would disrupt the preferred ambience of comfort and communal integration. Not so, however, for a collection of individual villas, where homogeneity is an aesthetic and social drawback, after all who wants to pay to live in a very expensive villa that looks just like the one next door?

    Domestic architectural expression is thus predicated upon being different to the neighbours, not necessarily more flamboyant—decorum and neighbourly politesse are at a premium in the leafy suburbs—but individual identity must be established. In the well-established process of villa construction in the Good Class Bungalow precincts of Singapore, each house is erected in accordance with the owner's timetable and desires on a specific and circumscribed site, but when a more spacious, sub-divisible plot of land is ripe for redevelopment, a meeting place for individual expression and collaborative benefit can be realised. Such a scenario became possible when the family that owned a hilltop site in the Dalvey neighbourhood decided to convert their gardens into a set of residences. The location was dress-circle Singapore, with views to the towers of Orchard Road and the forested slopes of Bukit Timah, and the sloping plot could be neatly segmented to accommodate six Good Class Bungalows in addition to the family's existing villa at the crown of the hill. The owner/developer family (to be referred to as the DalveyS family), who owned the land and had built the villa in 1954, approached Ko Shiou Hee of K2LD, an architect who actually had experience

FIG. 3 The six architects/designers behind Lien Villas Collective (from left to right) Edmund Ng, Ko Shiou Hee (MP), Terence Chan, Franklin Po, Randy Chan and Colin Seah

in coordinating a collaborative housing scheme in Singapore, which had gained much publicity and critical kudos.

The Lien Villas Collective (FIG. 2) had been completed in 2010, and located in a small valley rather than on a hilltop, it comprised five villas (and one extension) designed by an intriguing selection of young Singaporean architects (FIG. 3). The project was publicly referred to as 'No Boundaries' and made an idealistic virtue of its fenceless communal landscape, which featured geometrically assertive pieces of architecture that played off one another's adjacency. Ko's masterplan retained and extended the Lien family's historic villa at the top of the valley's gentle slope, and placed two rows of houses on either side of shared gardens and pathways on the grounds of the family's orchard. As a student in the United States and as a teacher in the NUS architecture program, Ko had always evinced great interest in the notion of collaboration: "I fundamentally disagreed with the traditional university process of creating hero architects," and the implementation of the Lien Villas Collective (FIG. 4) came after many years of setting collaborative design projects for his students at NUS. He allocated identically sized adjoining plots to each student in the course and was intrigued to note the disparities of intention: "Many students wanted to 'safeguard' their own issues and were very protective of their creativity, while others were more concerned with the overall result... they took into account the need for shared amenities and connections."

FIG. 4 Model of the Lien Villas Collective

More than ever convinced by the benefits of collaboration in architecture, Ko learned a lot from the Lien Villas project, where he had observed a degree of 'self absorption' at work and the practical shortcomings of a resolute 'no boundaries' approach. As the ground level fell steeply rather than gently at Dalvey Estate, the topography did not lend itself to such communal intimacy, and he invited established architects who were unlikely to indulge in formalistic over-experimentation on such a prime piece of real estate. This is not to say that Ko actively discouraged architectonic expression, but he was mindful of the value of the end result: "The owners, the building contractors, the residents and their staff, not to mention the gardens and the environment... all their needs had to be assessed and put in place. We could not be too idealistic and we had to respect the occupants' privacy." Ko was also cognisant of the general apprehension that property developers felt in regard to such communal architectural endeavours: "It hardly ever happens because ego gets in the way. When the architects get selfish, the developers lose interest," and he was determined to deliver a collection of houses that satisfied his clients as well as the architects.

THE DALVEY ESTATE: PLANNING FOR HARMONY

Patrick Bingham-Hall

FIG. 5 The Frank Brewer house at Dalvey Road

During Singapore's interim period of the 1950s, when British control was waning and independence was looming, the DalveyS family purchased a large parcel of plantation land on Dalvey Estate, a low rise to the northeast of the Botanic Gardens. The area was thinly populated, with market gardens and plantations cohabiting with military encampments and educational campuses. A most venerable form of housing stock was to be found nearby in the Black and White House enclaves of Goodwood Hill and Adam Road, wherein high-ranking colonial functionaries could sip their gin and tonics on the verandahs of Tudor-style mansions built in the early 20th century. Dalvey Estate itself was distinguished by a wonderful two-storey pitched-roof bungalow, designed by Frank Brewer (FIG. 5) in the 1930s, which adapted the arts and crafts architecture of Edwin Lutyens and Charles Voysey to the climatic demands of the tropics, and it was used for many years as the residence of Singapore's president. The DalveyS family built a relatively humble villa on their site, which adjoined that of the Brewer house, and as the years went by the area became quite densely settled, although the neighbourhood retained a semi-rural atmosphere, surrounding by university playing fields and gardening nurseries.

  The Dalvey area had become one of Singapore's most desirable residential locations, and the DalveyS family asked K2LD Architects to subdivide their land in the manner of the Lien Villas Collective, which also had an existing villa in need of restoration. According to the decreed Good Class

THE DALVEY ESTATE: PLANNING FOR HARMONY

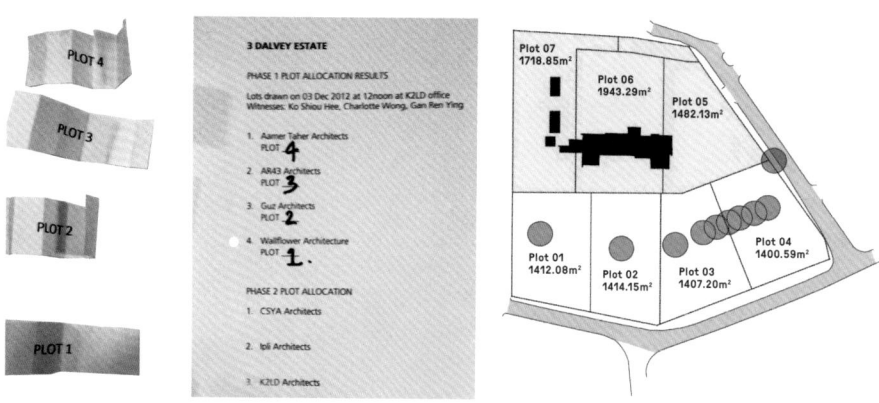

FIG. 6 Drawing lots for the seven plots

Bungalow spatial ratios for the moneyed districts of Singapore, the Dalvey Estate site could be sub-divided into seven plots, including that of the original house, and Ko Shiou Hee invited five architects, along with K2LD, to draw lots (FIG. 6) for their piece of land. The owner had specifically requested that ipli, the sixth architect, would be responsible for the restoration and alterations of the 1950s villa, as the practice had built up a reputation for its reinstatement of Singapore's mid-20th-century architectural history.

Although each of the sub-division plots (FIG. 7) had a markedly different topography and orientation, the selected architects were content with their lottery results and amicably resolved any issues of privacy requirements, height limits and services accessibility. K2LD's masterplan could be viewed in two halves and was built that way, with a set of three villas sitting on a plateau above four villas on the main street frontage below. The ground-plane gradation was only slight, but it was imperative that the lower houses did not block the views and eastern breezes from the three hilltop villas, so they were capped by flat roofs whilst the three up above were distinguished by their pitch. As the family was still residing in the 1950s villa, the four lower houses were built as the first stage, and each of their plans was influenced by the presence of seven majestic tembusu trees, which had to be protected at any cost. As it transpired, most of the trees were diseased and in their death throes, but the plans of the villas were duly prescribed by arboreal deference, and the resultant arrangement was pleasingly airy and spacious,

FIG. 7 Early discussions in progress

with all four villas content to relax and nestle into their hillside landscape.
   Construction began on the lower half of the site two years before the second stage, and a different approach and ambience can be detected on the two levels. The designs of the four lower villas are acutely aware of the formal geometric constraints of their street-front sites and the placement of the towering tembusu trees, to the point where the two southernmost houses both adopted a C-plan to embrace the trees, which also formed the centrepiece to the orthogonal armature of the two to their north. Even though the tembusu linkage on the lower-level first-stage has technically disappeared, the three second-stage villas on the hilltop feel less integrated with each other, and they have less sense of enclosure, as their western boundary on the edge of a small steep hill is relatively undefined. The overall environment of the seven-villa estate is agreeably harmonious, and one appreciates the almost subliminal attachment and the sense of shared purpose across the breadth and depth of the site, between each of the houses and their gardens. One is always aware that the compound is essentially unlike the arbitrary collection of exclusively designed Good Class Bungalows which comprises the affluent zones of Singapore, yet it does not demand excessive architectural scrutiny or interpretation. The Dalvey Estate is quite simply a successful property development that asked its architectural participants to contribute to a venture wherein the resultant whole needed to be greater than the sum of its parts.

COLLABORATIVE HOUSING: AN URBAN ANOMALY

"Architects should be required to respond to their neighbours at all times and at all scales. As the city becomes more congested, Singaporeans are placing increasing value on their privacy and architects must respect that. It would be good if we could always work together, along with planners, landscapers, environmentalists and engineers to build a more practical and harmonious way of living. We can be inventive as well as being respectful, and in order to do that we should be collaborating."

Ko Shiou Hee

THE SEVEN VILLAS: EXPRESSION AND DEFERENCE

Patrick Bingham-Hall

Although the plots assigned to the seven architects were of a similar size, they each had to contend with a singular set of constraints and opportunities. The overall site fanned out from the west to the east down a gentle slope to the main street, with a short cul-de-sac forming the northern border. The two southern plots adjoined the lovely shady grounds of the 1930s Frank Brewer house, whilst the two northern plots were relatively exposed to the street and the unremitting sunshine. The two central plots on the lower level formed an environmental extension of the timbered shadiness of their southern neighbour and the Brewer house, whilst the central hilltop plot, which contained the original villa, had been more or less defoliated and its environment presented a stark contrast to its southern and eastern neighbours. The masterplan referred to the plots in a sequence from 1 to 7, which spun as a pinwheel around the overall site from the southeast to the southwest, and it would be appropriate to describe the architects' intentions in the same fashion.

When viewed as a collection, which is admittedly rather difficult to do given the generally intransigent approach to privacy enacted by the residents of private houses, the Dalvey 7 Estate does represent an affirmation of Ko Shiou Hee's belief in architectural collaboration. Such collaboration does not mean two, three, or even seven, architects crowded around a single drawing

board or hooked into: single-purpose WhatsApp group, but a selection of individual architects producing individual designs that take those of the others into account, and which prioritise the context and serviceability of the project as a whole. The variety of expression at the Dalvey 7 Estate is of course delightful, as every architect had an established pedigree, but it was also quite expected, as they all stayed true to their identifiable styles and strengths. Nobody rocked the boat, apart from ipli with their whimsical deconstruction and reconstruction of the original house, but that approach was actually anticipated and, one might say, quite necessary, in order to centre the disparate yet deferential expressions of the surrounding villas. Whether subsequent such exercises can flourish in an urban context will depend upon the availability of such relatively large swathes of land, and the willingness of a Ko Shiou Hee to coordinate the process. Dalvey 7 Estate, like the preceding Lien Villas Collective, drew its strength from its concurrency and mutual spontaneity. Unlike so many gated communities on the fringes of Asia's cities, where construction proceeds incrementally and the architects have a conceptual tabula rasa, these two Singaporean projects reflect the spirit of a specific time and they display a sense of communal cohesion, which must be welcomed by residents and by the architects themselves.

SEE THROUGH HOUSE

WALLFLOWER ARCHITECTS

01

The See Through House by Wallflower Architects occupies a sublime patch of land, a virtual extension of the Brewer house's lawns and shaded by a row of conserved Tembusu trees. Wallflower's domestic architecture has demonstrated a gradually evolving parti, which in essence comprises two permeable pavilions flanking a courtyard that serves as an indoor/outdoor living space. Through this gesture, Wallflower's subtle geometric and modern architectural language takes a contextual approach towards the 1930s bungalow as an exercise on contrast and reciprocity, acquiescence and respectful appreciation. It is a deliberate contrast between the Brewer's House 'object-making in the landscape' model against the See Through House's 'space-making in the landscape' model. The lengthy elevations of the pavilions are elegantly composed of timber battened screens, which pivot to provide extensive cross-ventilation and shading as and when required. Wallflower's strategy of maximising the passive cooling and shading of a tropical house has created an architectural signature of low-slung horizontality and a veiled sense of depth, augmented by fleeting changes of mood, dependent upon any adjustment to the serried rows of battens.

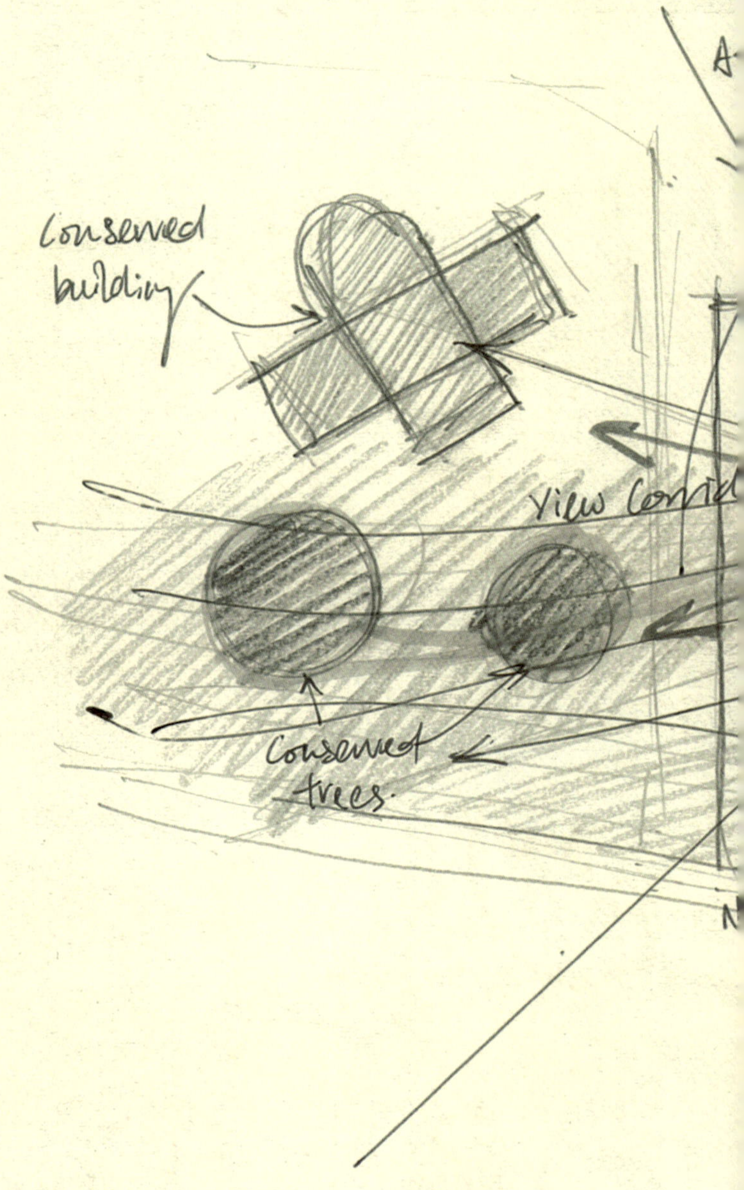

Conserved building

View corri[dor]

Conserved trees.

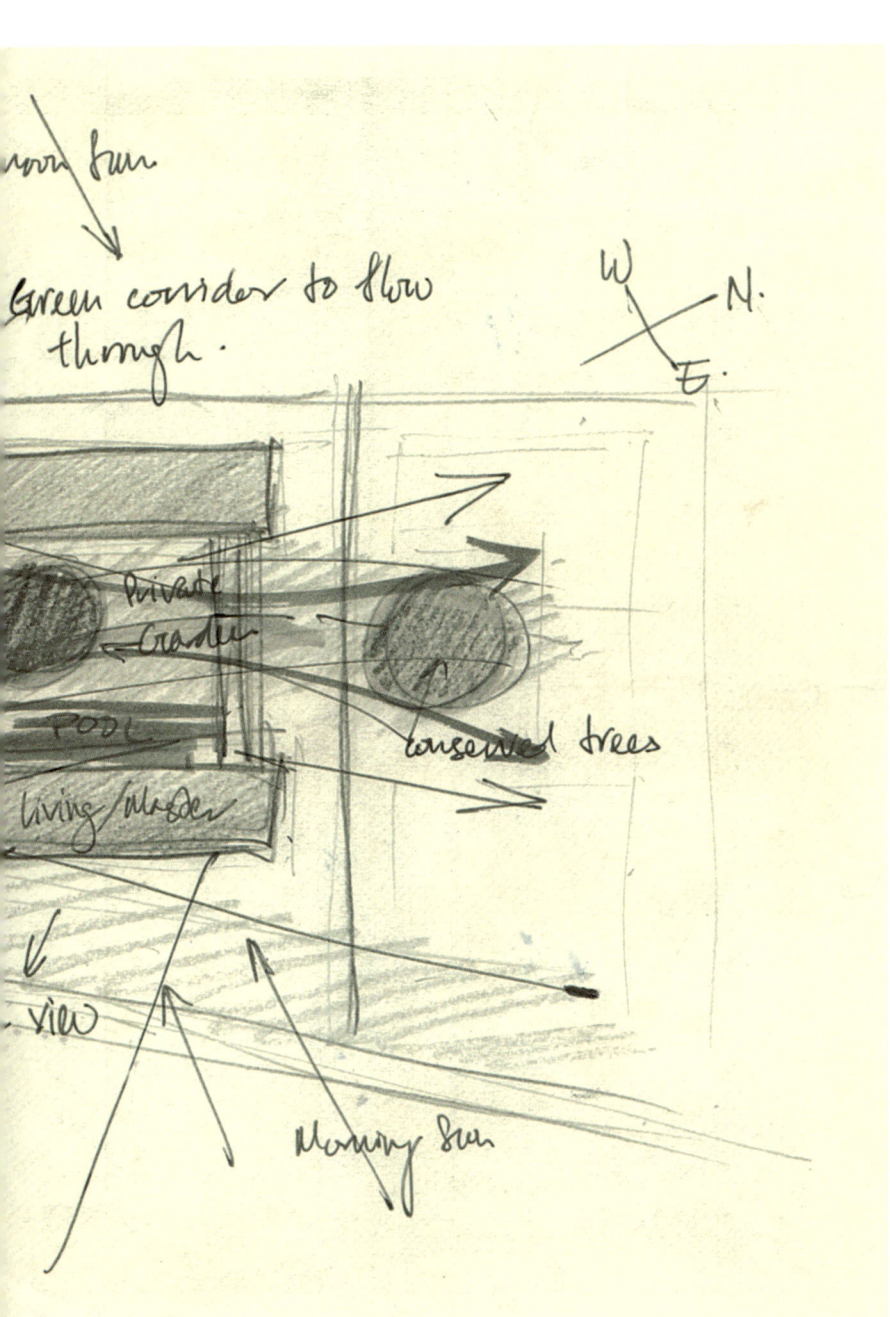

Massing Model

11/1/13

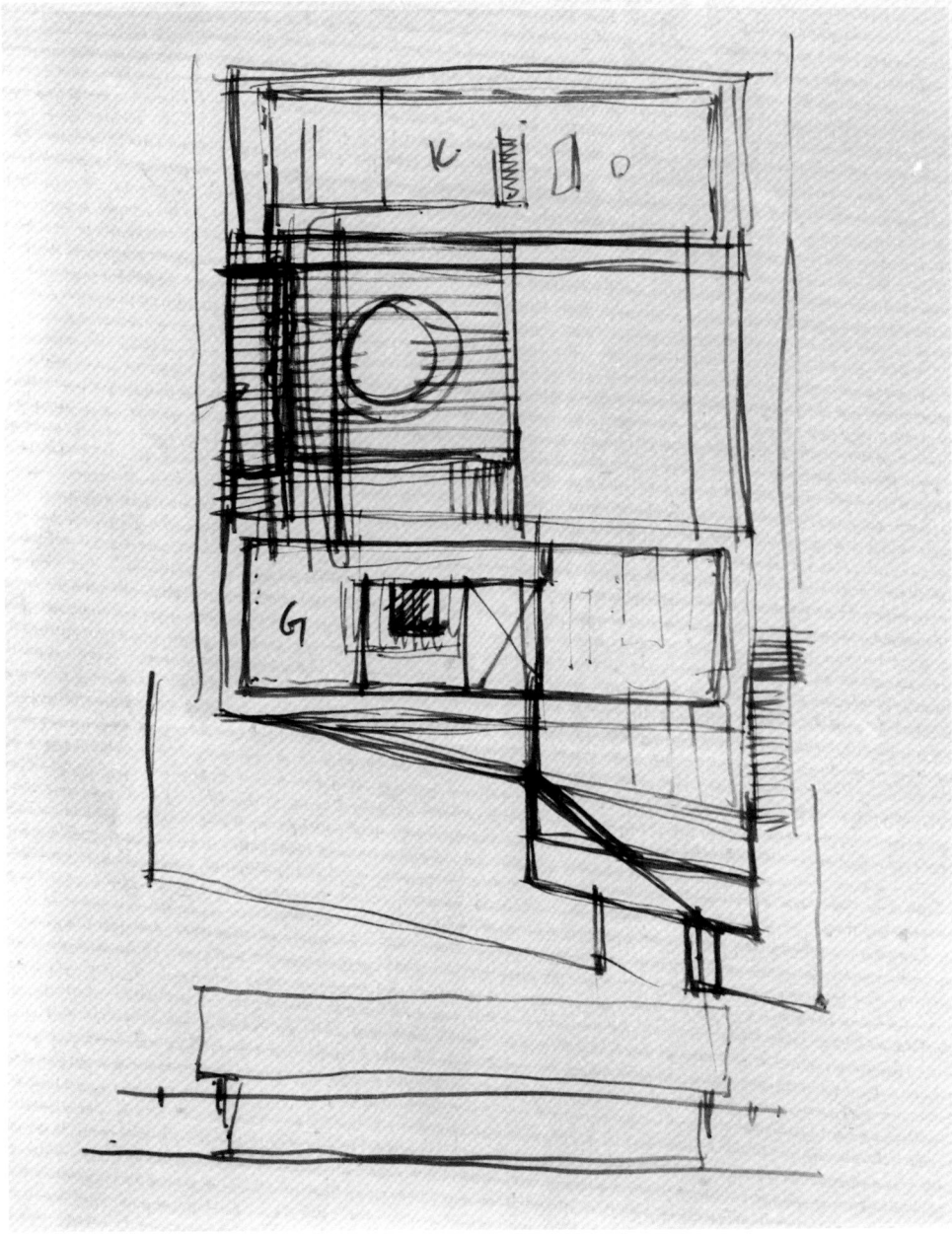

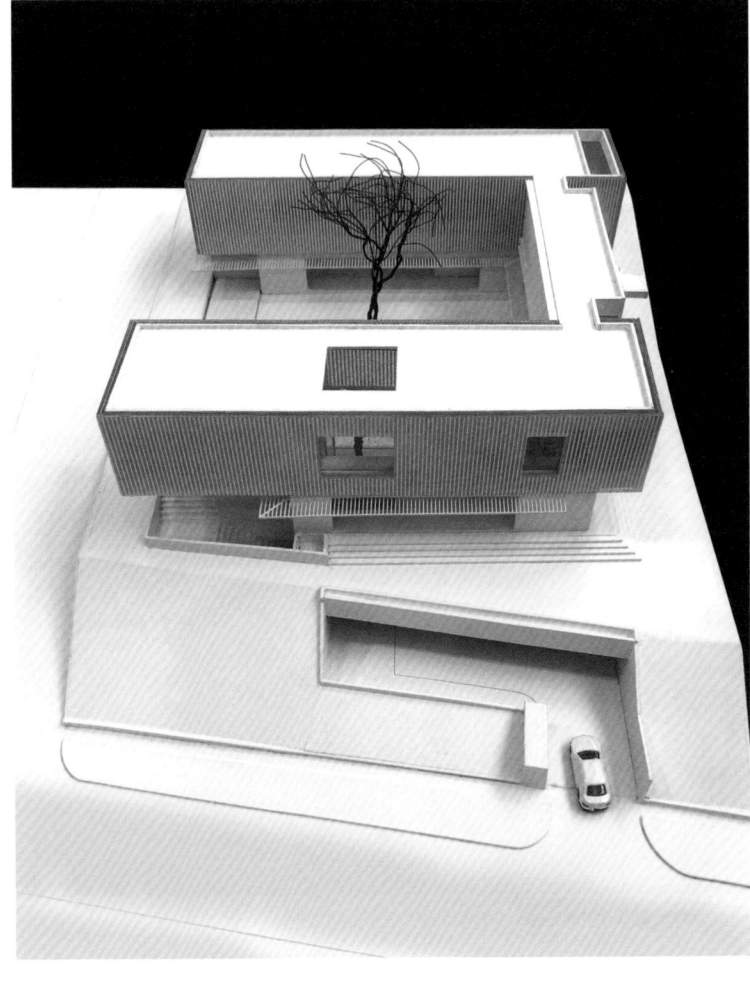

The adoption of concrete walls, timber shuttered windows, and a geometrically simple and understated expression, underscores the desire to defer to the conserved colonial house sited directly across the See Through House, once the residence of a former president of Singapore.

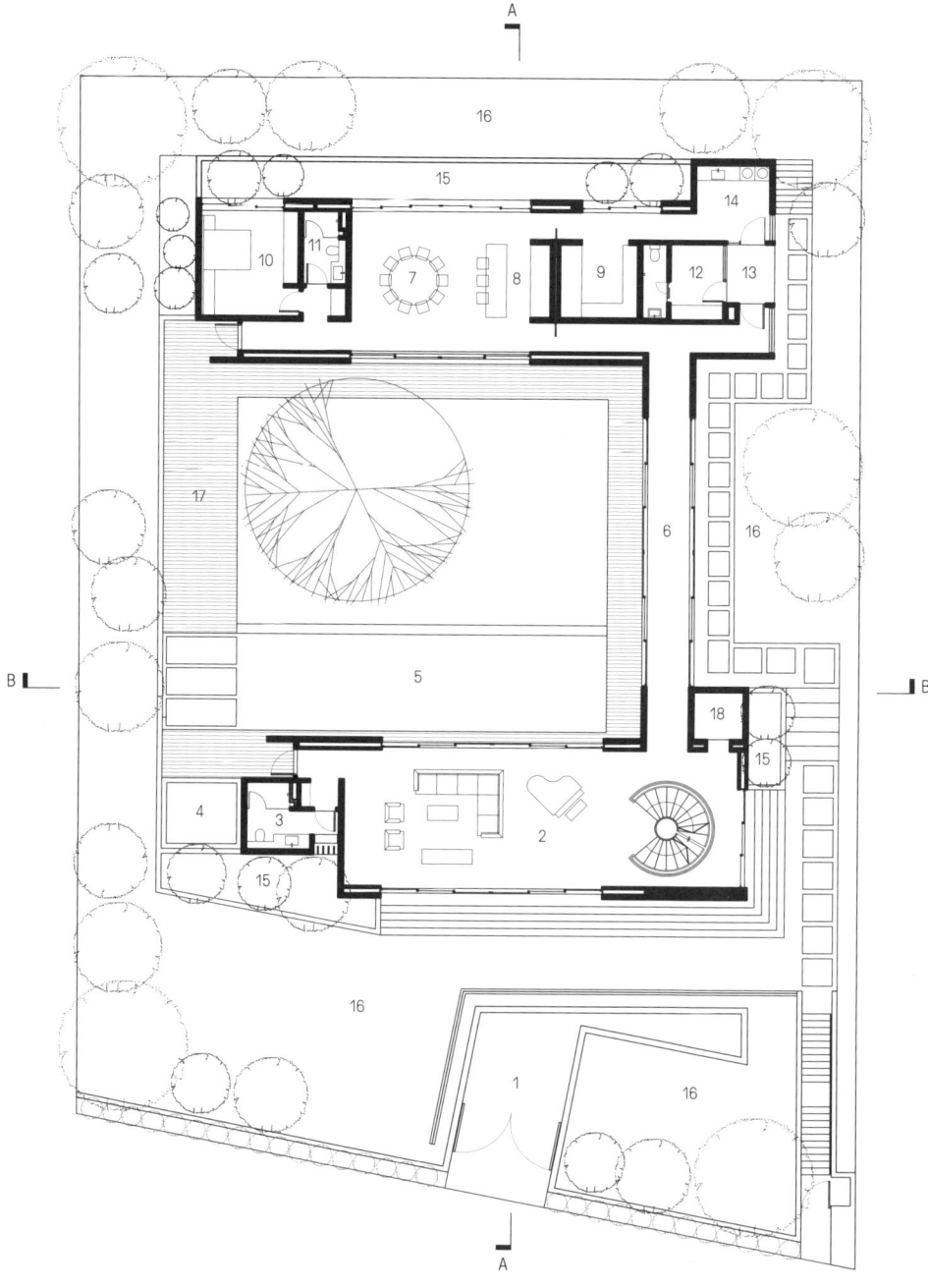

1st storey

1. driveway below
2. living
3. power room
4. outdoor shower
5. swimming pool
6. linkway
7. dining
8. dry kitchen
9. wet kitchen
10. guest room
11. guest bath
12. utility room
13. yard
14. laundry
15. planter
16. landscape garden
17. outdoor deck
18. lift

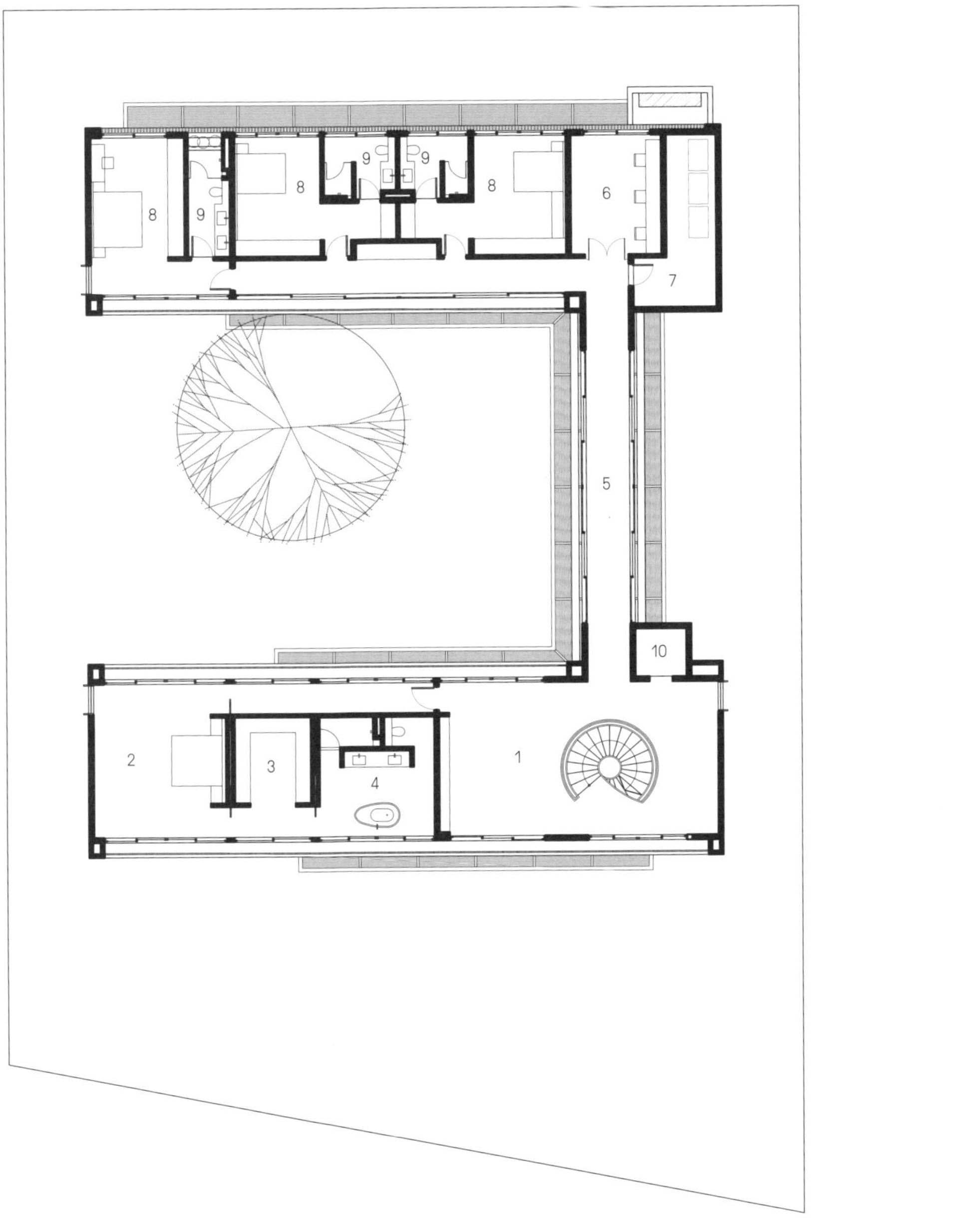

044–045   SEE THROUGH HOUSE   WALLFLOWER ARCHITECTS   PLOT 01

1. family room
2. master bedroom
3. walk in wardrobe
4. master bath
5. linkway
6. study
7. m&e
8. bedroom
9. bath
10. lift

2nd storey

A lone Tembusu tree protected under a conservation act, sits squarely in the middle of this plot.

The courtyard enclosure is conceived as an intimate outdoor room and the central core of an atrium-style house.

Breezeway between both wings of the house allowing uninterrupted passage of breeze through the courtyard.

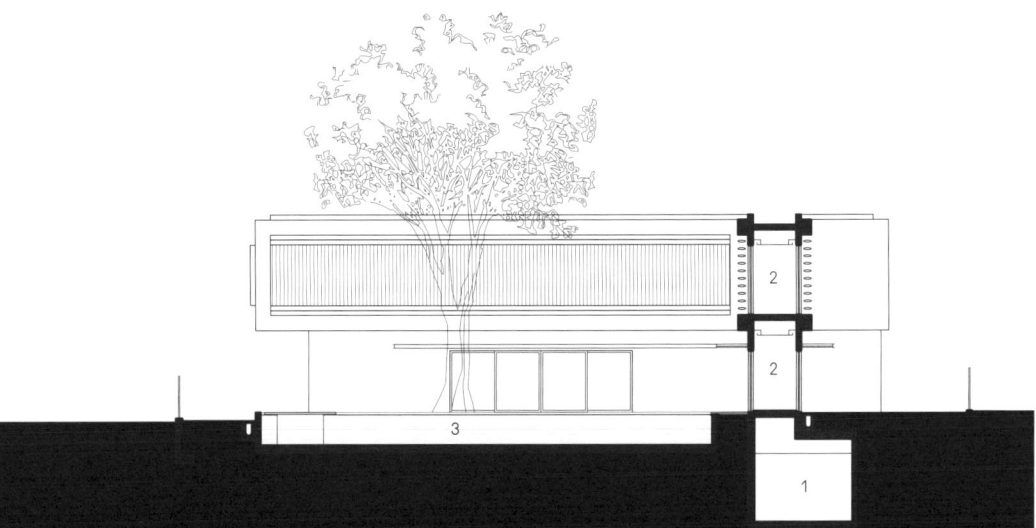

1. basement
2. breezeway
3. swimming pool

Cross section B

050 – 051   SEE THROUGH HOUSE   WALLFLOWER ARCHITECTS   PLOT 01

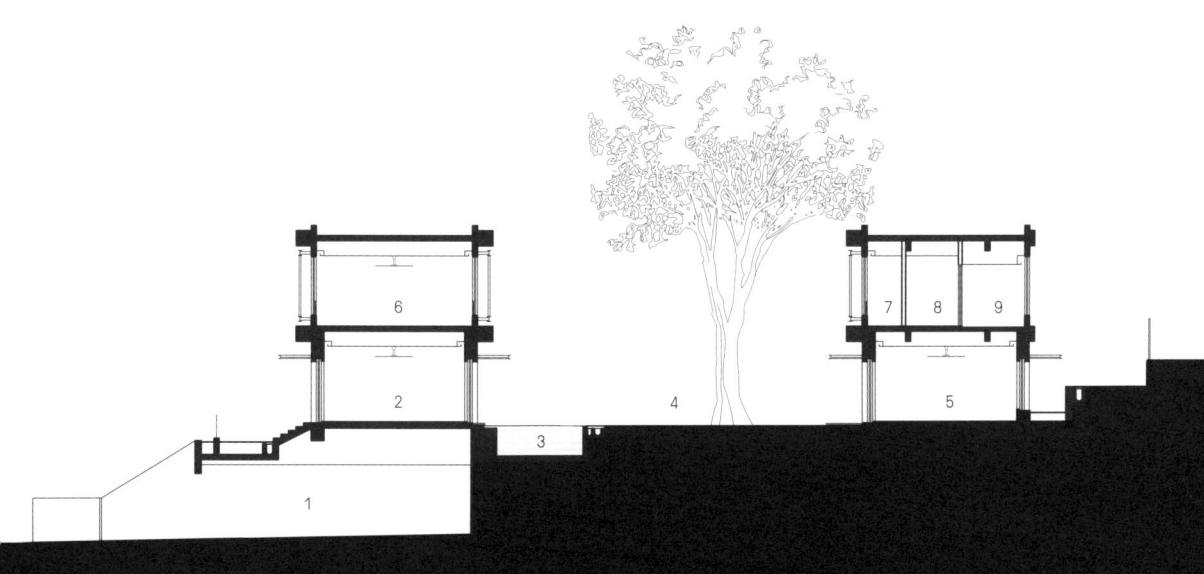

Cross section A

1. carporch
2. living
3. swimming pool
4. courtyard garden
5. dining
6. master bedroom
7. walkway
8. bedroom
9. bath

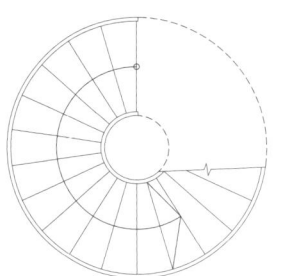
Basement plan

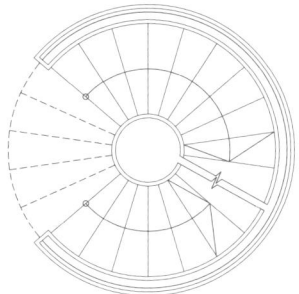
1st storey plan

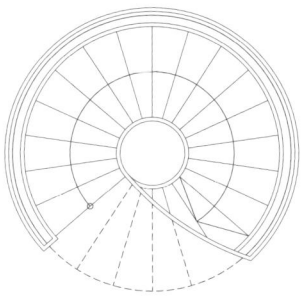
2nd storey plan

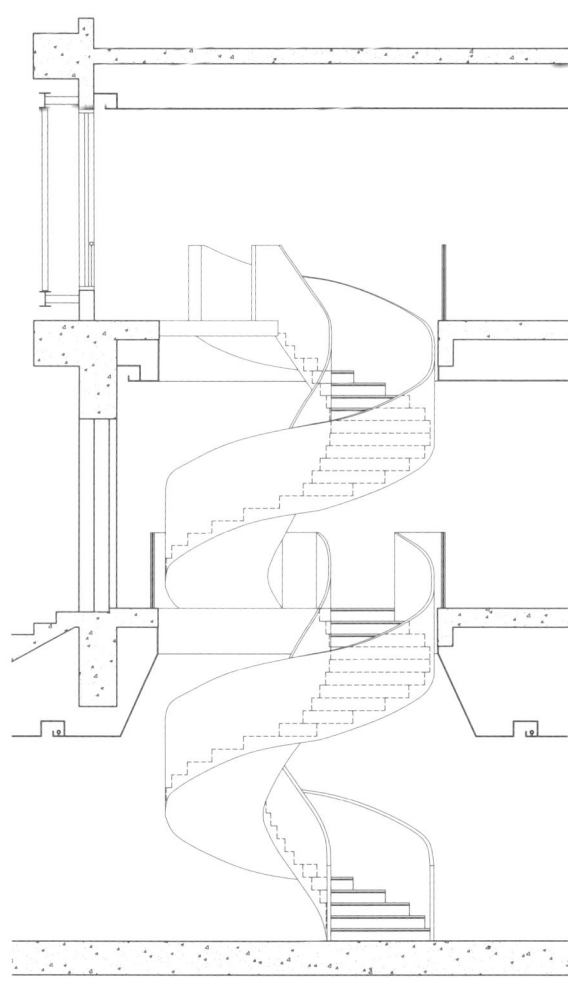
Spiral stairs section

The steel, glass and timber spiral staircase with integrated step lights linking basement, first and second storey.

Details of operable sunscreen.

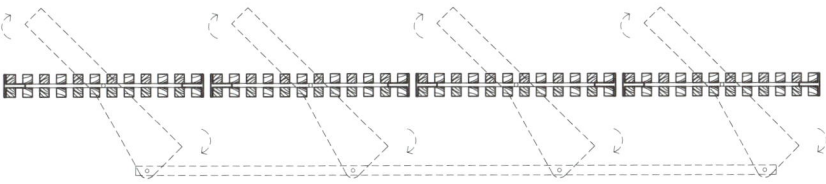

Timber screen detail

Screened corridor leading to bedrooms.

Second storey breezeway.

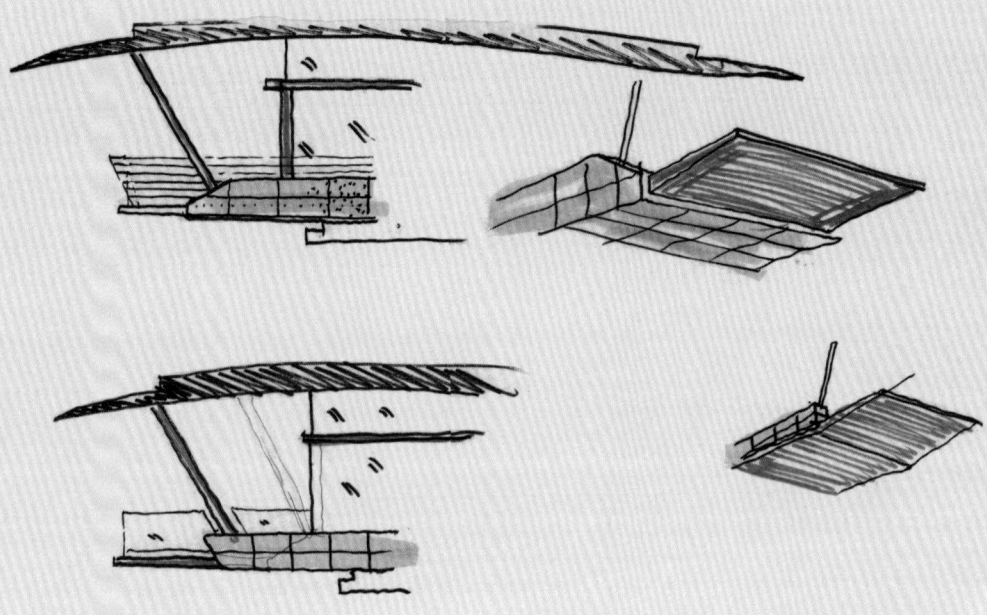

PROJECT

SAIL HOUSE

ARCHITECT

GUZ ARCHITECTS

PLOT

02

As with all four of the first-stage houses, the Sail House by Guz Architects was built on a flat site, on a platform raised as a podium well above the level of the street. Guz took full advantage of this lofty aspect to design a house whose extravagantly cantilevered wafer-thin roof looks like it literally has taken sail, soaring out from its well-treed gardens to catch the winds blowing from the east. Guz Architects has produced a notable oeuvre of such nautically inspired houses, but their significance does not reside so much in their metaphorical symbolism as in their environmental intention. With an elemental yet inimitably graceful timber composition, each house is calibrated to encourage all cross-ventilation possibilities, and the luxuriant landscaping is always accorded the same attention as the architecture: the structure and the gardens are as one. With a C-shaped plan, the Sail House encloses a courtyard with a single tembusu tree. This plan has been a parti of long standing to an architect immersed in the pleasures of tropical living.

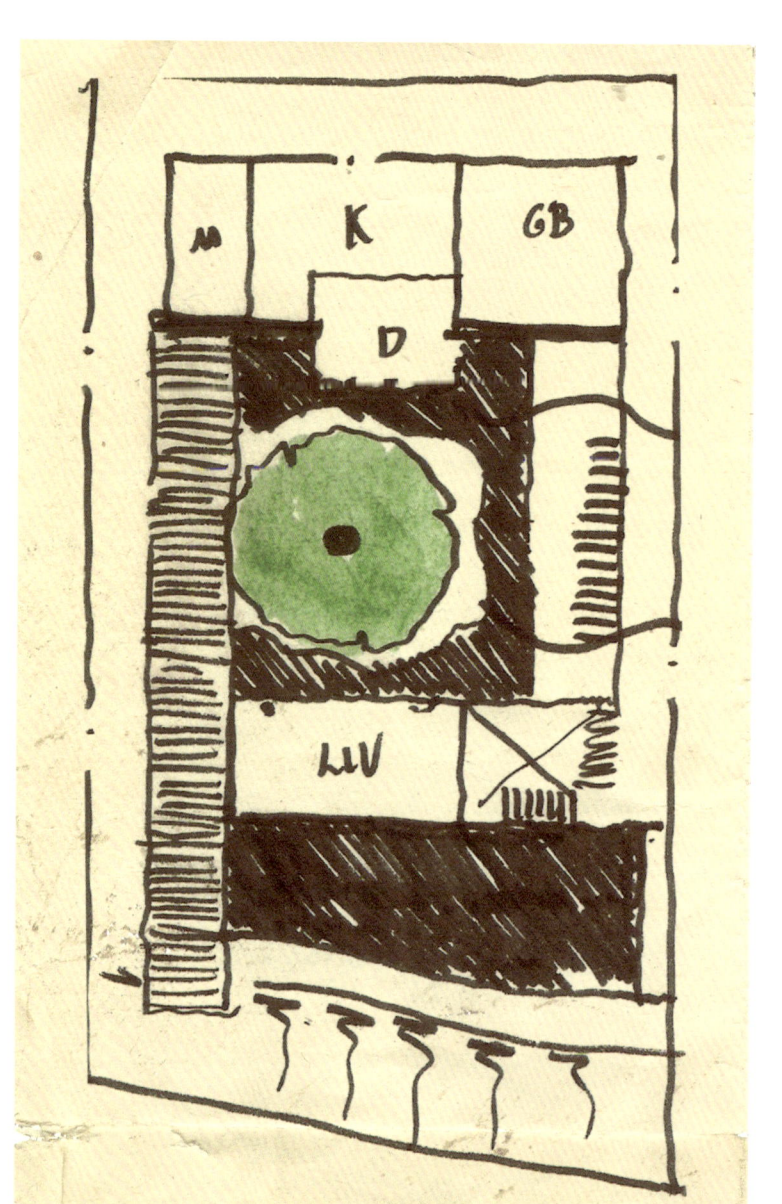

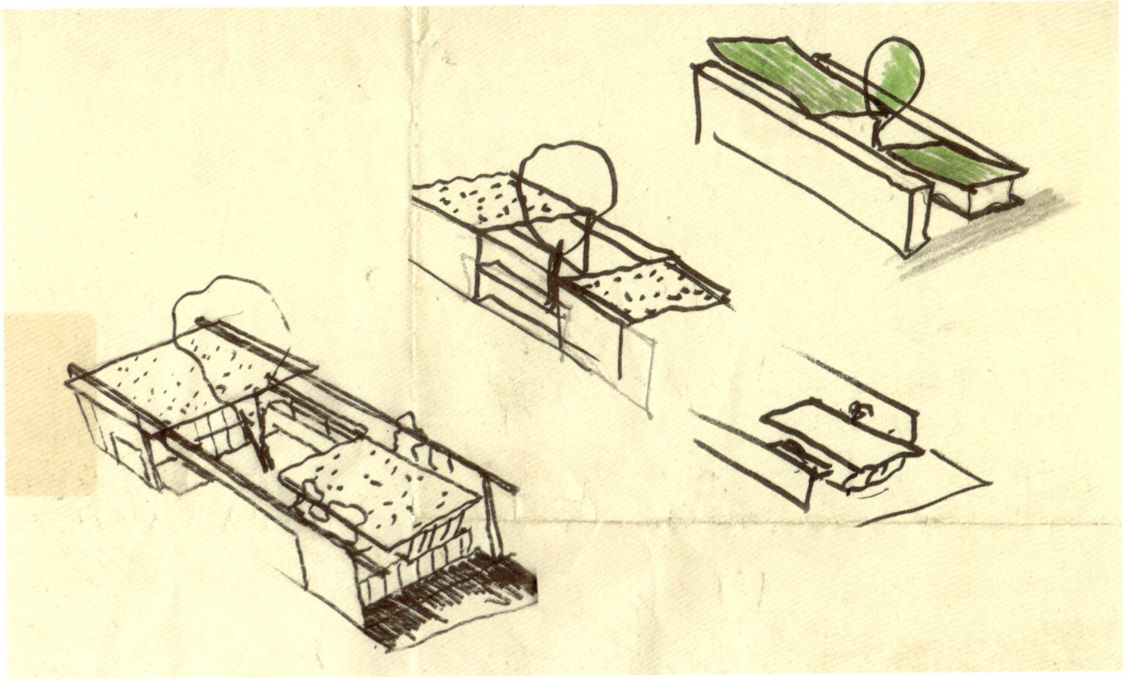

062–063 SAIL HOUSE GUZ ARCHITECTS PLOT 02

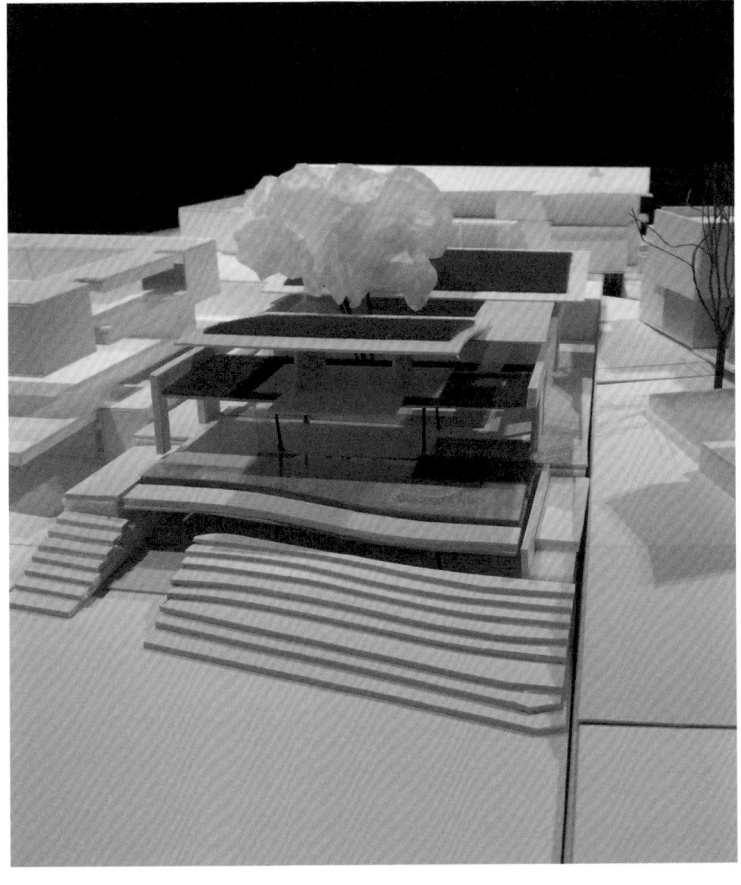

View of floating cantilevered master bedroom.

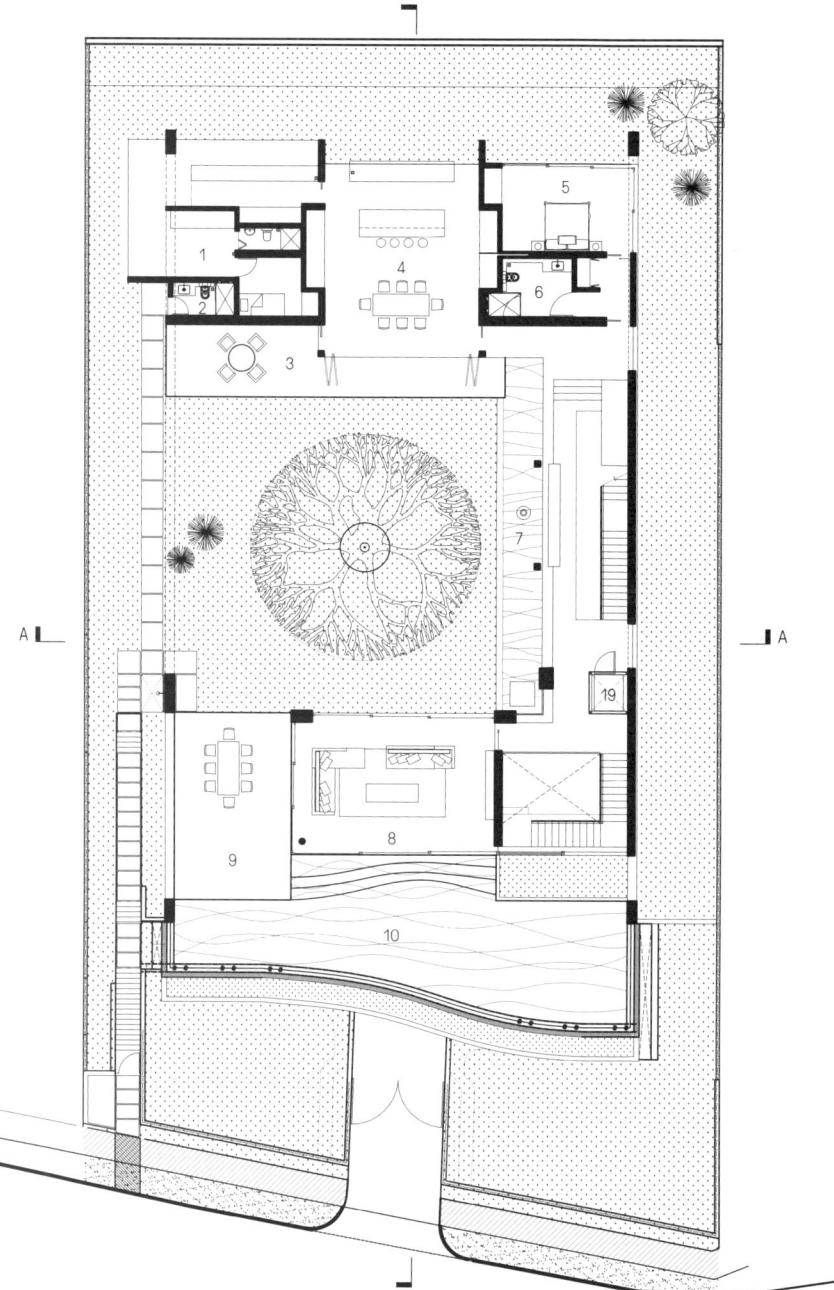

1st storey

1. laundry area
2. pool changing room
3. breakfast deck
4. dining room
5. guest bedroom
6. guest bathroom/powder room
7. pond
8. living room
9. pool deck
10. pool

066 – 067　　SAIL HOUSE　　GUZ ARCHITECTS　　PLOT 02

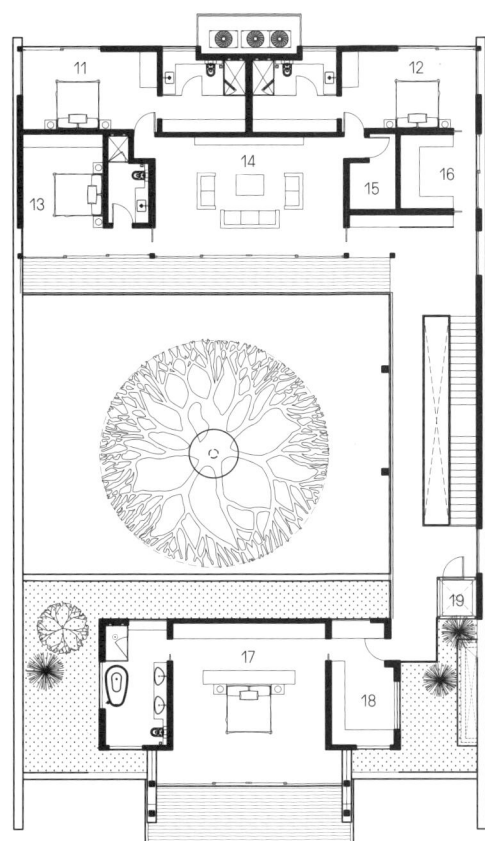

11. bedroom 1
12. bedroom 2
13. bedroom 3
14. family room
15. linen store
16. study
17. master bedroom
18. master study
19. lift

2nd storey

Main entrance stairway overlooking courtyard garden.

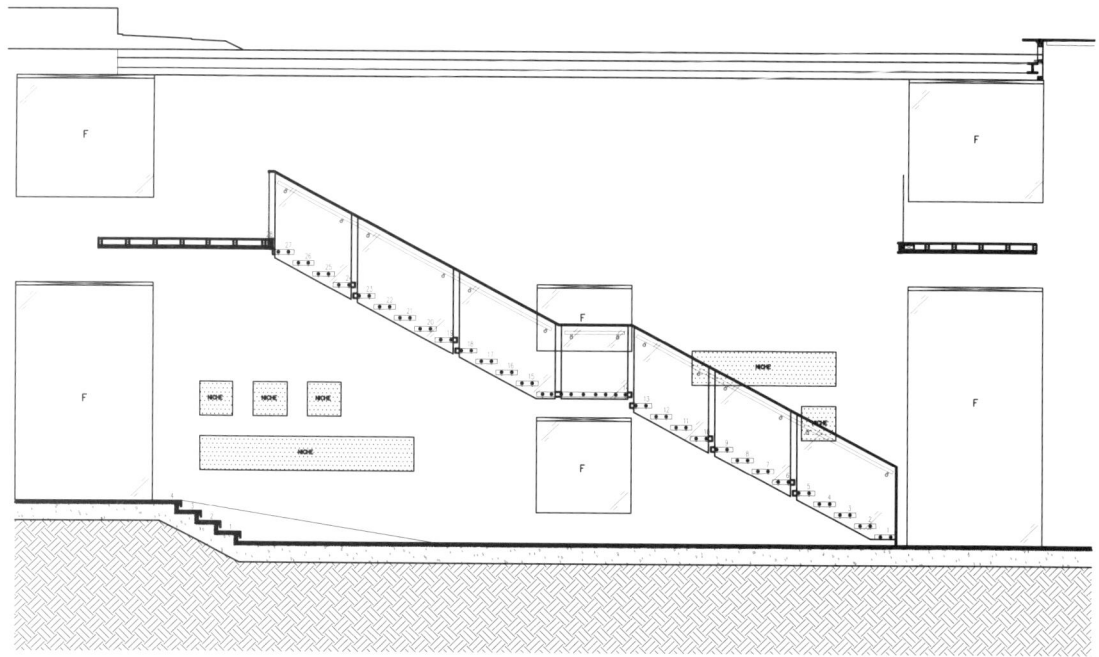

Main staircase detail

Bridge looking towards master bedroom suite.

Bridge overlooking central courtyard.

1. bridge
2. walkway beside pond and garden courtyard

Section A

074–075　　SAIL HOUSE　　GUZ ARCHITECTS　　PLOT 02

Top: Roof garden at master study.   Bottom: Infinity edge pool with planter.

Curved cantilevered infinity edge pool.

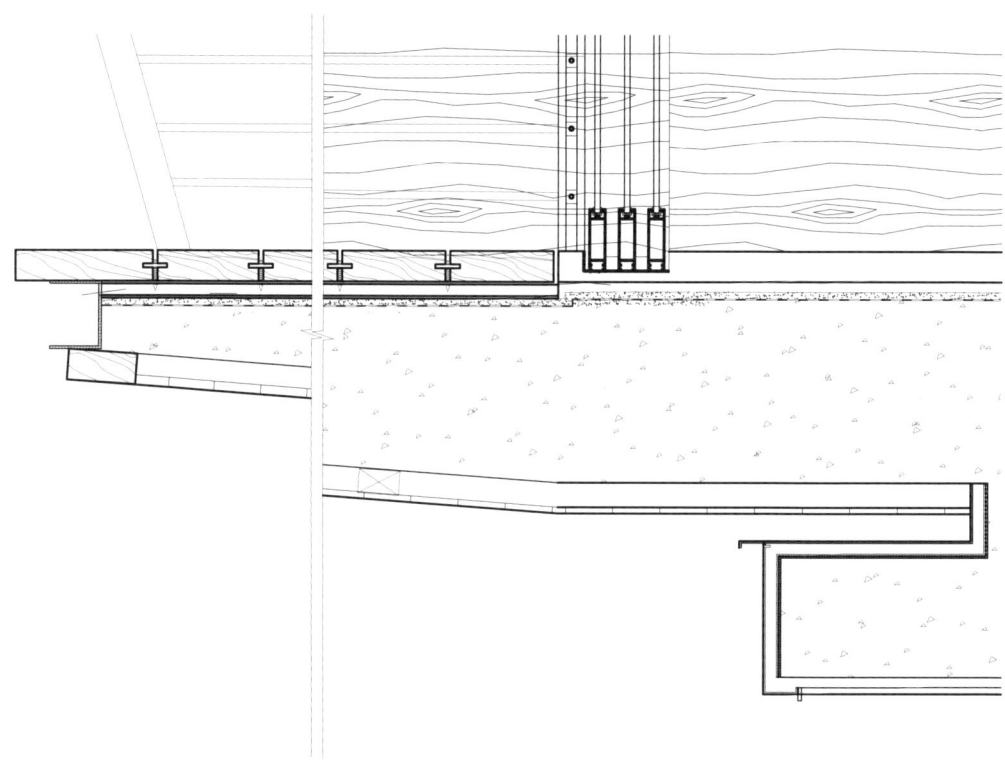

Balcony detail

View from master bedroom balcony.

Main driveway entrance.

PROJECT	ARCHITECT	PLOT
TEMBUSU HOUSE	AR43 ARCHITECTS	03

The Tembusu House, by ar43 Architects, was so named because the centre of the plot contained three tembusu trees in a row, so the architects had little option but to place two volumes on either side of the great trunks of the trees. This architecture is the most formally assertive in the Dalvey 7 collective, with a bold and overtly orthogonal massing that relies upon an interplay with the towering trees, and which set up its own dialogue with a contrast between dark-stained timber and concrete. The two main volumes (with double-height interiors) are surrounded by a series of precisely landscaped courtyards and pools, bisected by a passageway of clear glass sliding doors, which enables a visual continuity at ground level denied by the solidity of the second floor. The impact of the black-stained teak cladding is resolute and formidable, both relieved yet reinforced by a corresponding array of bright-white planar walls. The elevated white orthogonal volume that presents itself to the street is cantilevered – with the aid of a frosted-glass cylinder-as-piloti – above a swimming pool and deck in a manner reminiscent of the domestic work of Lautner, Niemeyer and Johnson, and the entire ensemble constitutes a sparkling essay in what has been termed 'tropical modernism'.

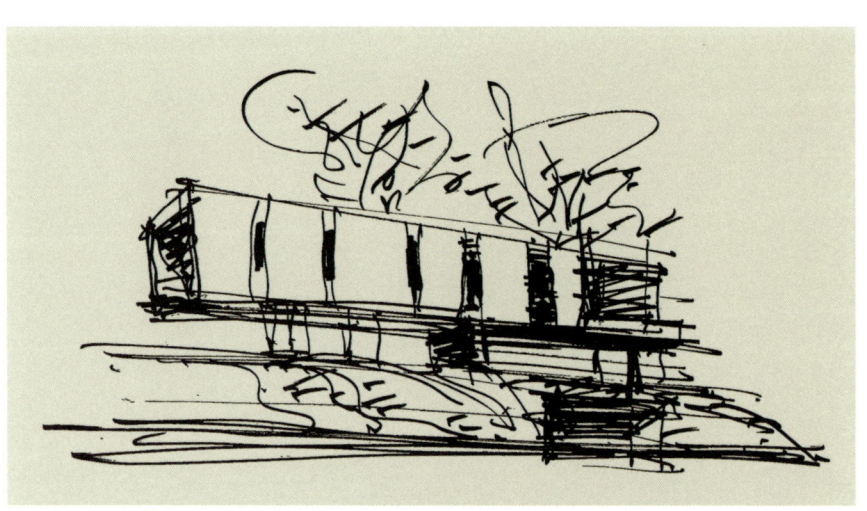

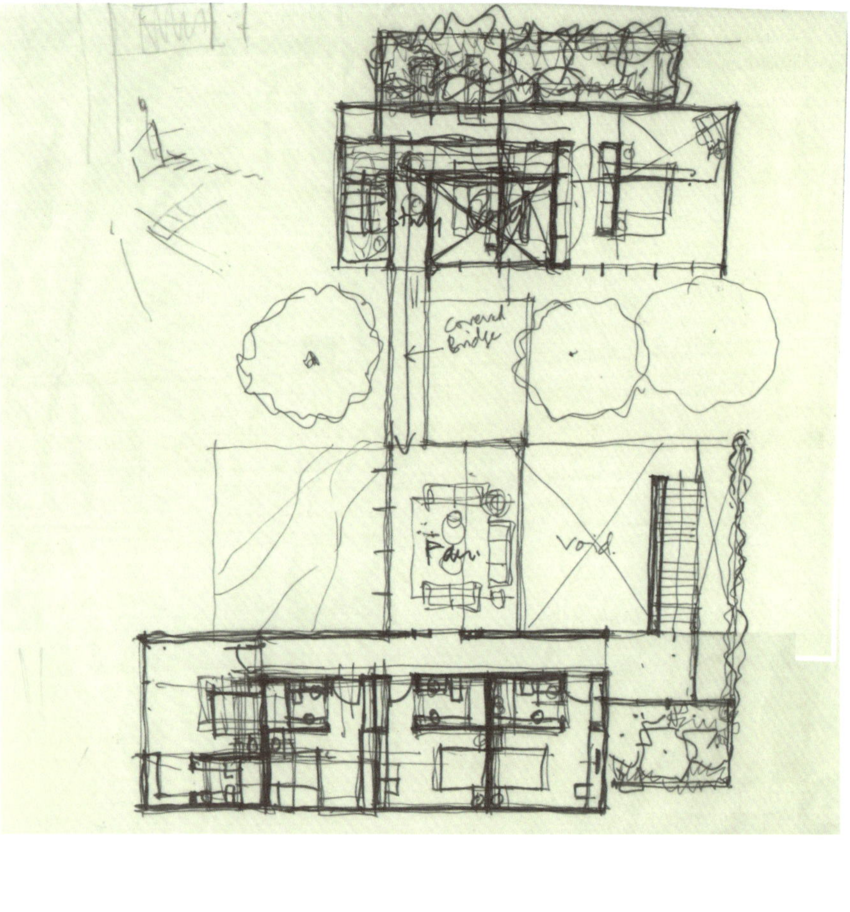
study
covered bridge
Fam.
void.

TEMBUSU HOUSE — AR43 ARCHITECTS — PLOT 03

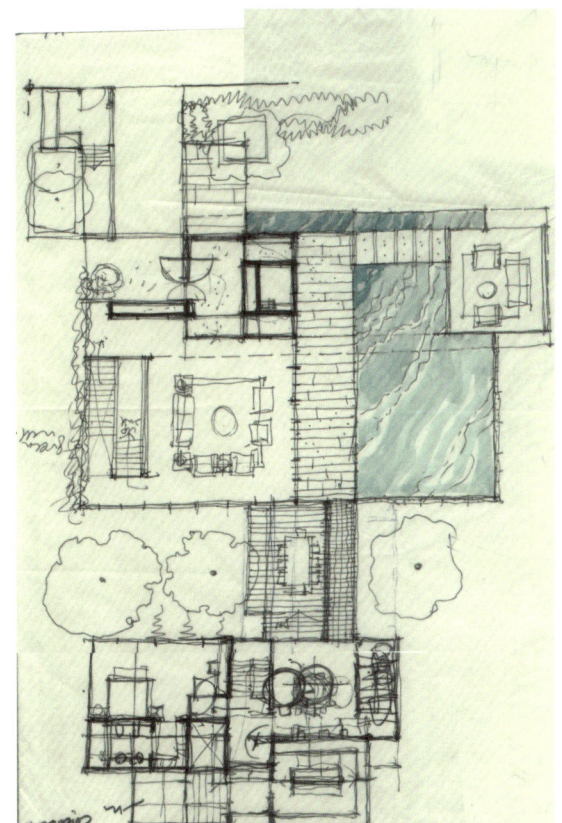
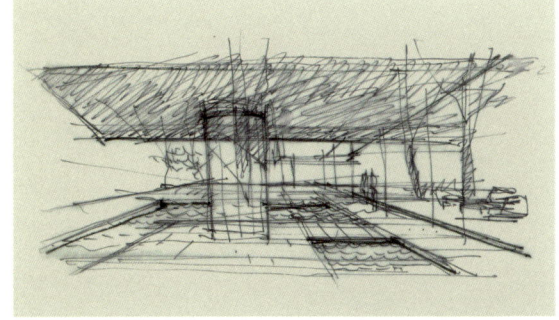
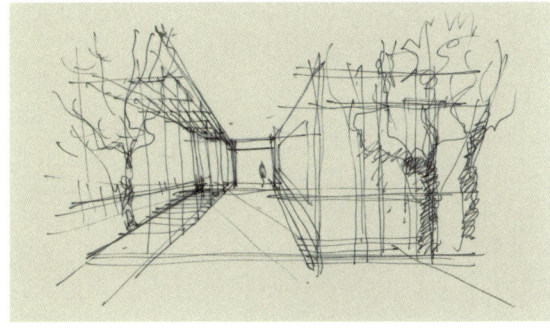

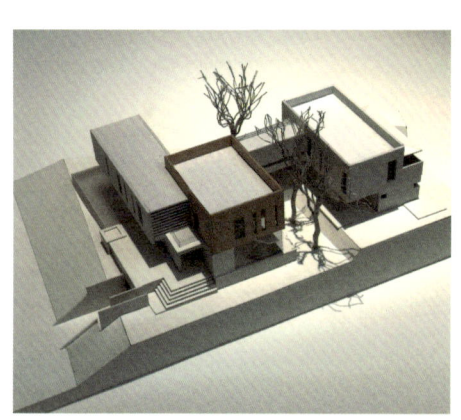

086–087 TEMBUSU HOUSE   AR43 ARCHITECTS   PLOT 03

Ascending to the main entrance terrace from the street level.

Side view from neighbour's garden.

View from the front slope.

In parallel with the front garden is the dramatic infinity pool and a sheltered jacuzzi.

The main grassy garden of the house centred by the magnificent Tembusu tree, towering over the play pool and timber deck.

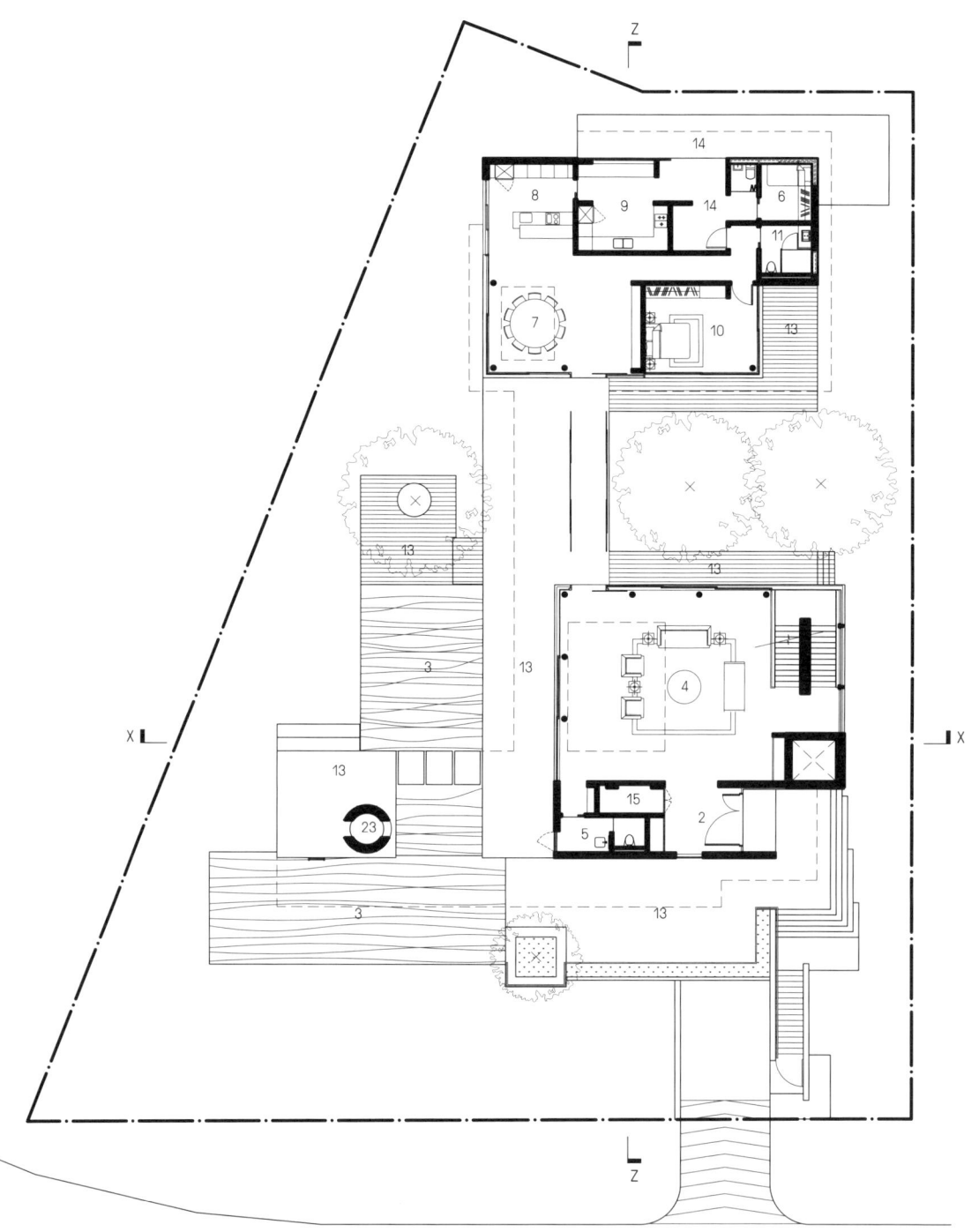

1st storey

094 – 095 TEMBUSU HOUSE AR43 ARCHITECTS PLOT 03

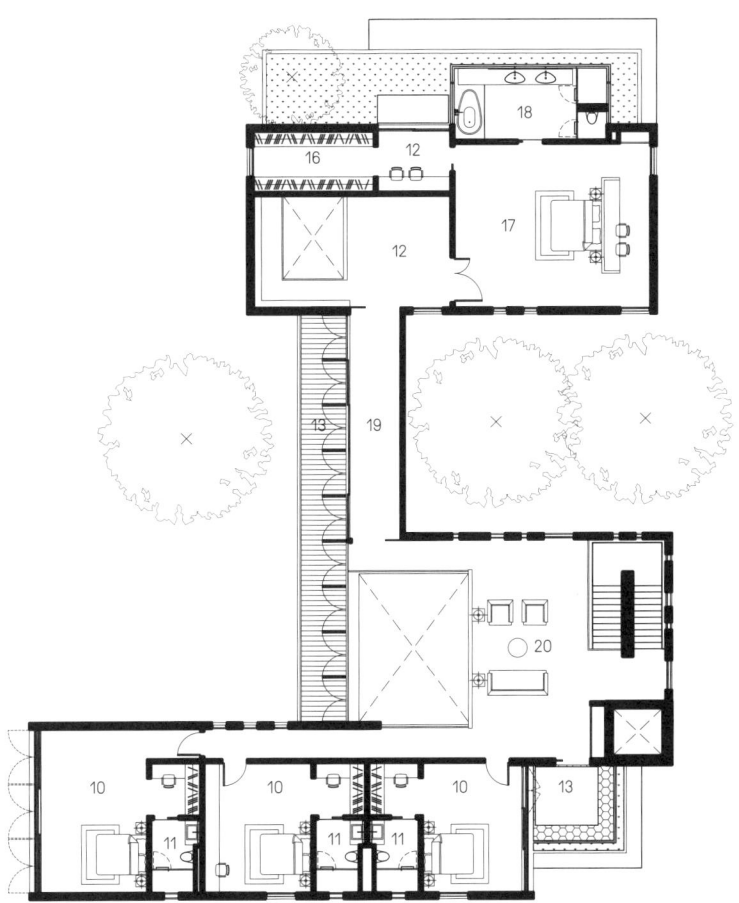

2nd storey

1. carporch
2. foyer
3. pool
4. entertainment/ living room
5. powder room
6. utility room
7. dining room
8. dry kitchen
9. wet kitchen
10. bedroom/guest room
11. bathroom
12. study
13. outdoor deck/terrace
14. yard/laundry
15. store
16. master wardrobe
17. master bedroom
18. master bathroom
19. gallery
20. family
21. hs shelter
22. services
23. outdoor shower

Front elevation

Right elevation

Side view of the central courtyard.

Section X

Towering Tembusu trees frame the facade of the timber cladded living room block, casting intricate shadows over the courtyard and living room.

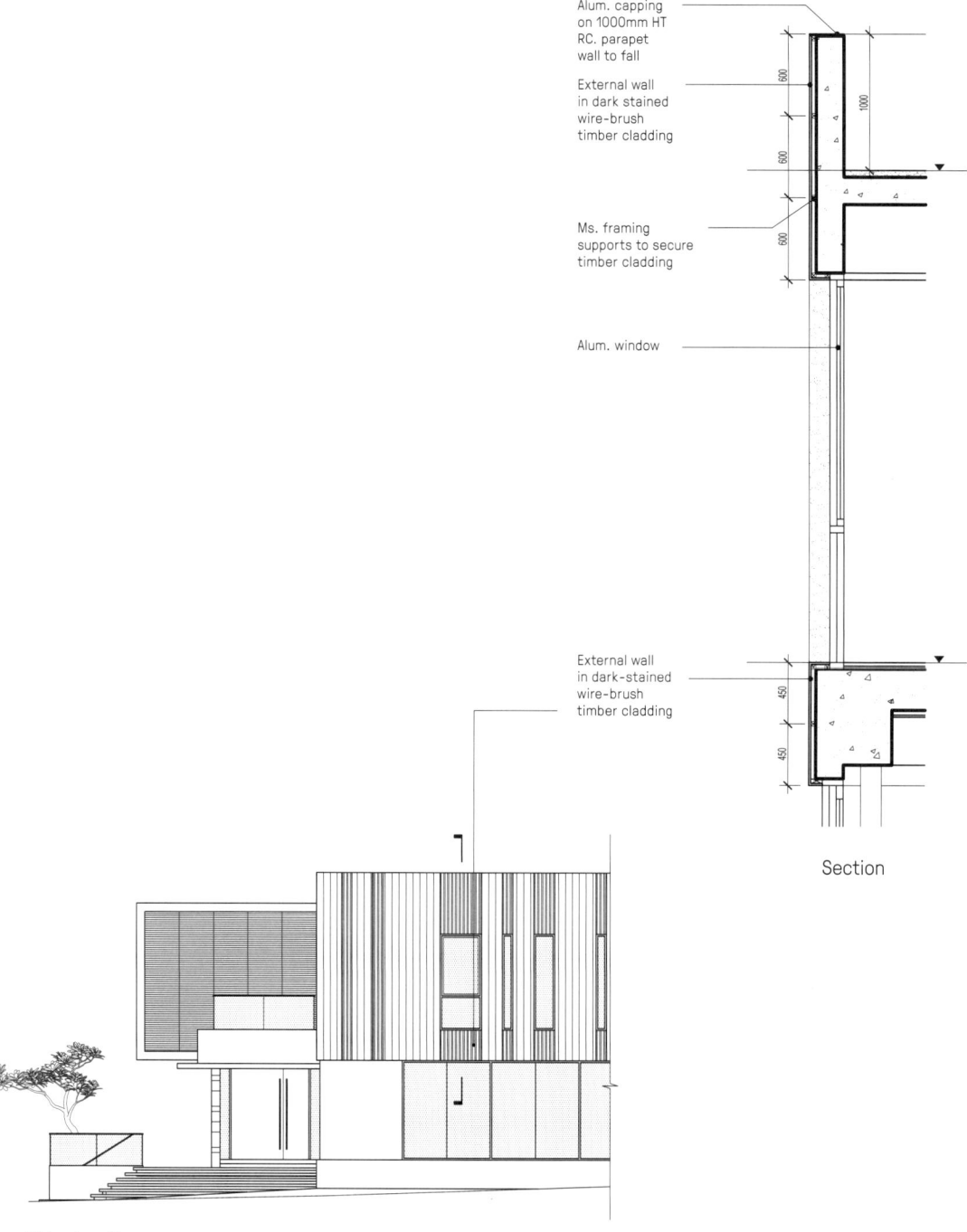

Dark-stained timber cladded wall, wire-brushed with rough grain and texture depicting the trunks of the Tembusu trees.

View of bedroom looking across the internal courtyard.

A glimpse of the courtyard from the internal staircase.

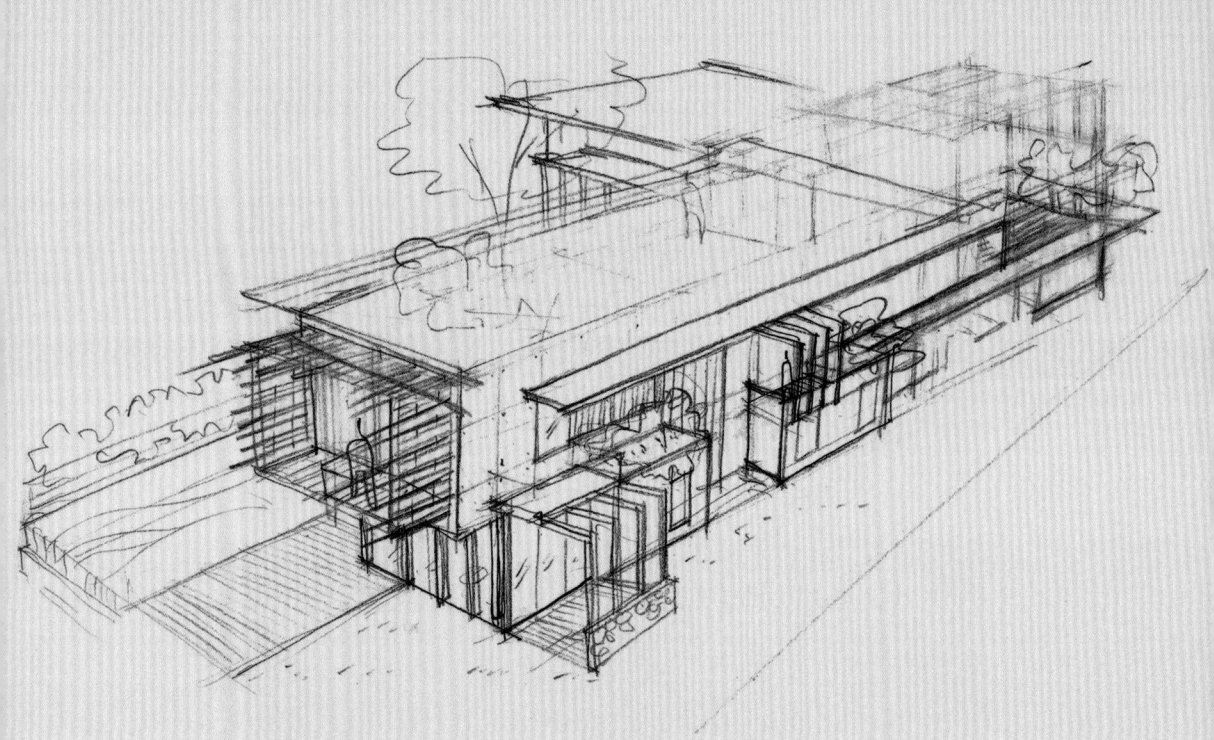

| PROJECT | ARCHITECT | PLOT |

GALLERY HOUSE

AAMER ARCHITECTS

04

Aamer Architects has produced a broad range of designs of Singaporean houses over the last twenty years, veering from the flamboyant and voluptuous to the elegant and well mannered. In keeping with the collective desire to not cry out 'look at me', Aamer chose the latter option for the Gallery House at Dalvey Estate, which sits upon an L-shaped plan that recedes from the strong massing of the Tembusu House to be braced by a wall that serves as a public buffer at the northeast corner of the overall site. Raised well above the street level and screened by a row of trees and hanging creepers, the external wall has a sober expression in white-painted concrete, establishing the right to privacy required by the potentially all-too-public Dalvey Estate site. The formal expression within the arms of the L plan is altogether different, and the architects have revisited one of their best-known earlier houses, at nearby Kheam Hock Road, for its delicate bipartite horizontal composition. The upper floors of the two wings are shielded by an array of honey-coloured vertical timber-lookalike aluminium louvres, whilst the living areas on the ground floor are completely transparent, opening out to the gardens through full-height sliding glass doors. A continuous sun-filled gallery, or circulation corridor, runs the full length of the two wings, looking out over timber decks, a set of pools and water features, and a large open lawn, to the city towers in the distance. The overall disposition is that of calm and charm, with an underlying intention to set the tone for the compound and 'protect' the neighbouring villas and gardens.

External view from road junction.

Al-fresco at poolside.

Poolview and movable vertical aluminium louvres.

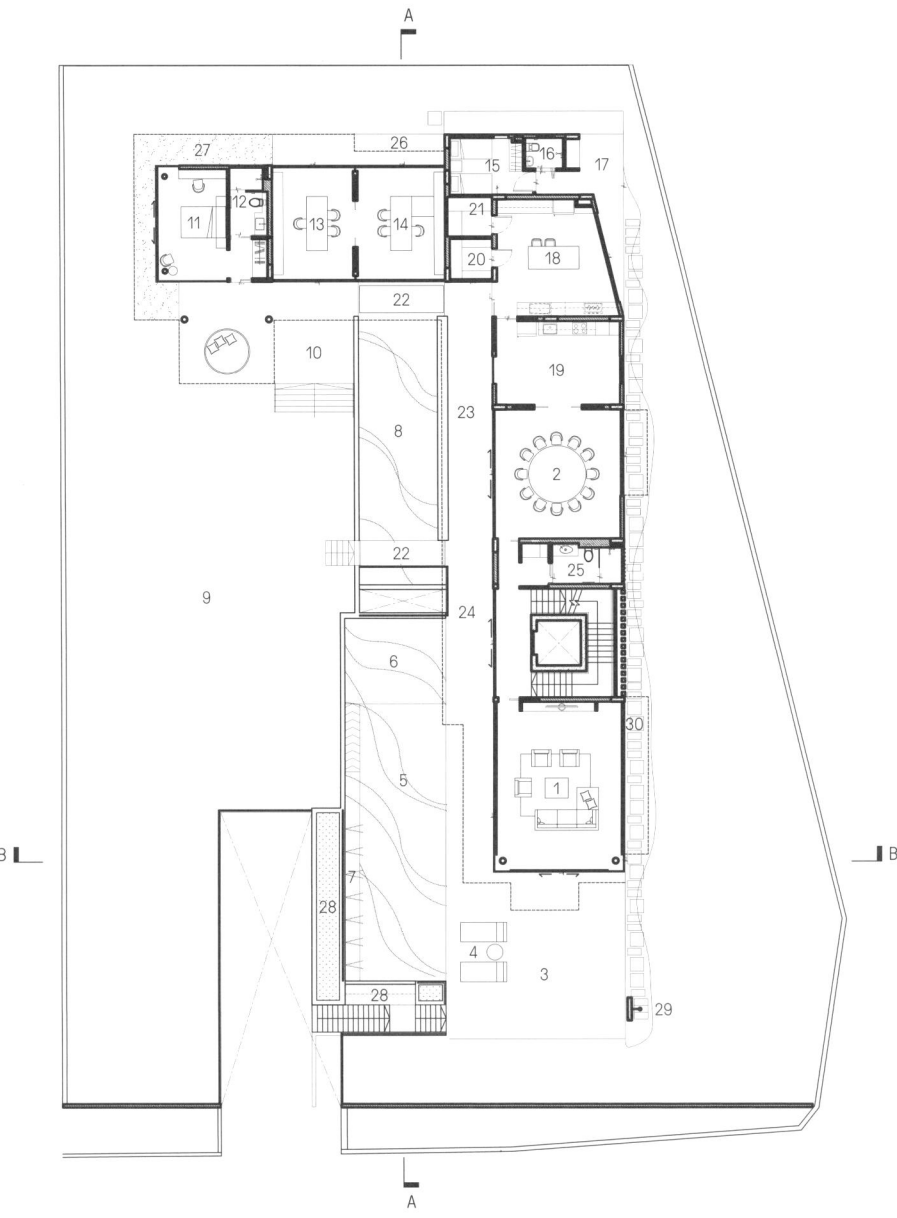

1. living
2. dining
3. bbq area
4. pool deck
5. 1200mm deep lap pool
6. 300mm deep wading pool
7. jacuzzi
8. 300mm deep pond
9. garden
10. guest lounge
11. guest bedroom
12. guest bathroom
13. master study
14. family lounge
15. maid room
16. maid bath
17. yard/laundry
18. wet kitchen
19. dry kitchen
20. wine cellar
21. store/larder
22. bridge
23. feature bench
24. feature wall
25. powder room
26. outdoor deck
27. loose pebbles
28. planter
29. outdoor shower
30. stepping stones

1st storey

GALLERY HOUSE — AAMER ARCHITECTS — PLOT 04

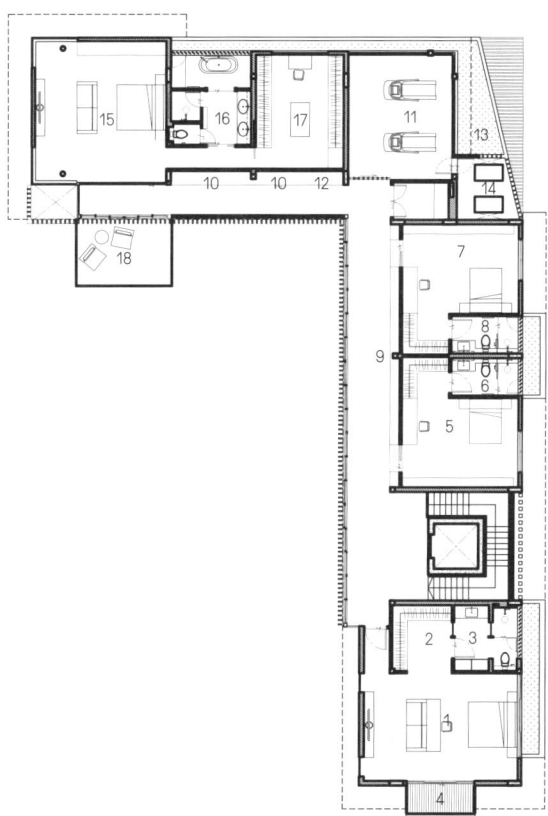

1. junior master suite
2. walk-in wardrobe
3. junior master bath
4. balcony
5. bedroom 1
6. bathroom 1
7. bedroom 2
8. bathroom 2
9. library wall
10. store
11. gym
12. sub-db unit
13. planter
14. ac condenser
15. master bedroom
16. master bathroom
17. walk-in wardrobe
18. open treetop lookout

2nd storey

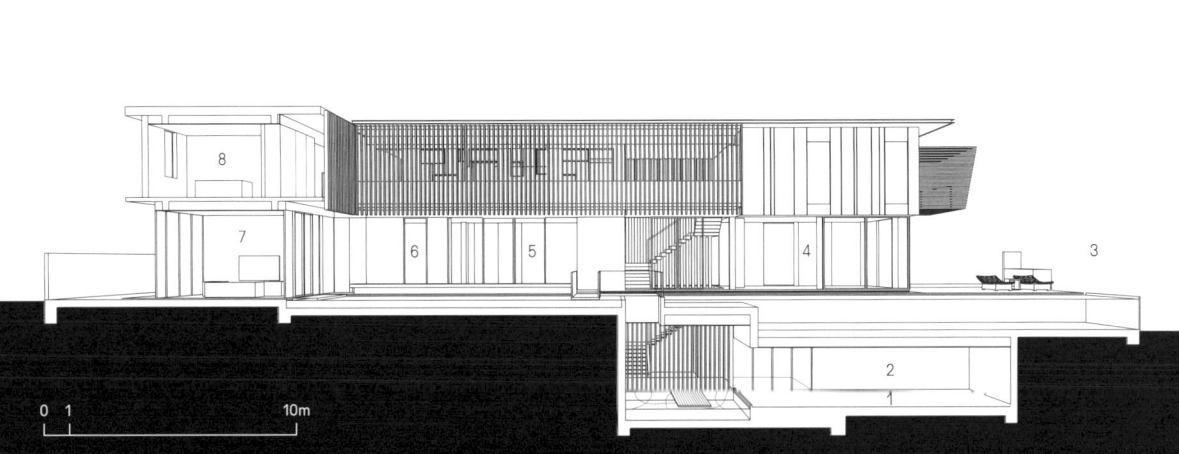

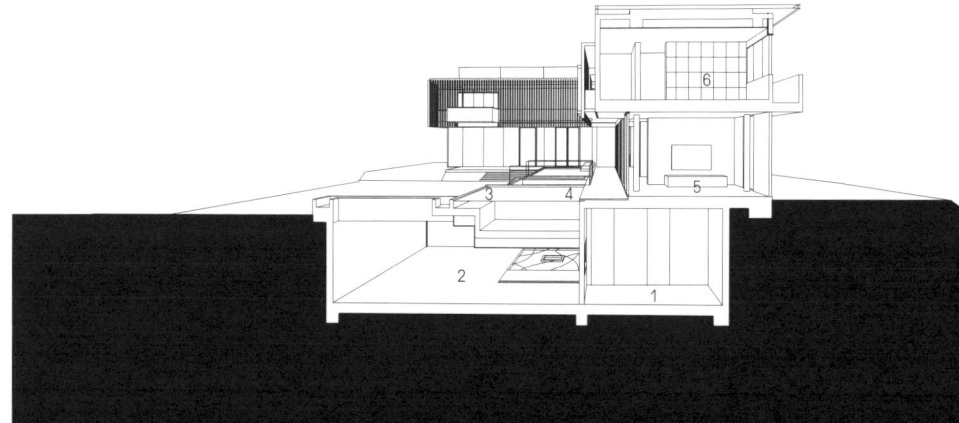

Section B

1. entertainment room
2. car porch
3. jacuzzi
4. lap pool
5. living room
6. junior master suite

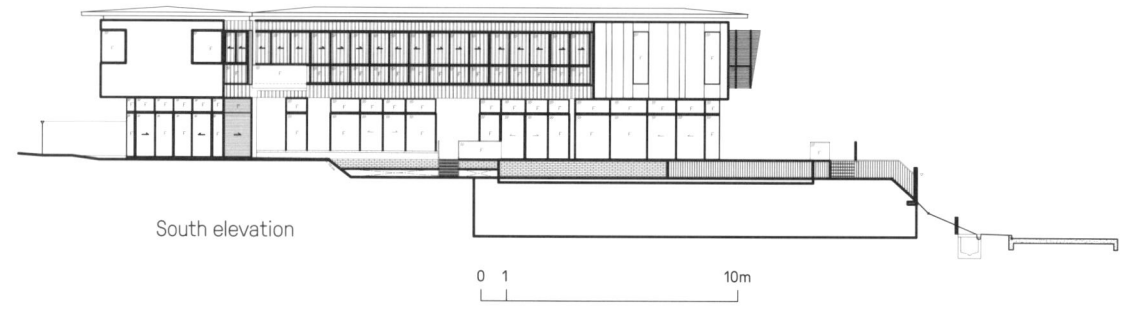
South elevation

0 1   10m

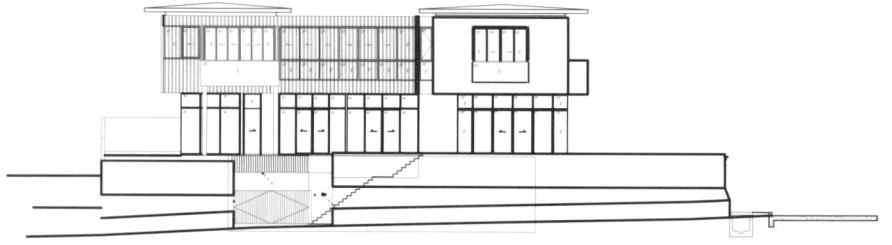
East elevation

Generous front lawn.

Open living room, space amplified by reflective ceiling.

Master bedroom with balcony.

Living room by the pool with distant city views.

Sun-filled corridor with movable vertical louvres.

Book shelves and storage lining the corridor.

View from the master bedroom terrace.

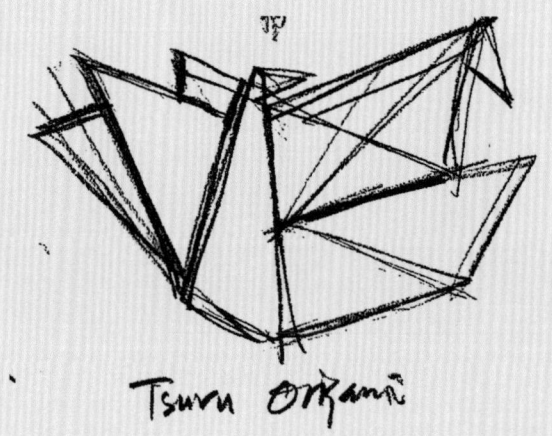

Tsuru Origami

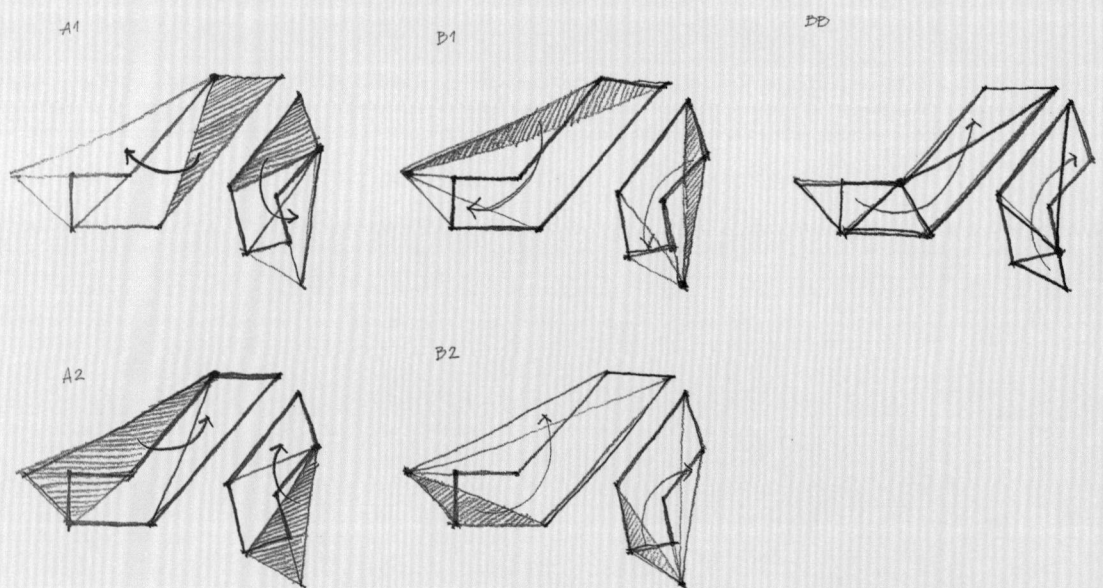

PROJECT

ORIZURU HOUSE

ARCHITECT

K2LD ARCHITECTS

PLOT

05

Directly above the Gallery House, on the exposed plateau of the site, the Orizuru House by K2LD also addresses the street with a protective set of white walls, but the expression is one of monumentality and geometric complexity. In terms of plan, section, and material appearance, the Orizuru House takes its cues from K2LD's Winged House, designed some five years earlier, and extends that language to form a more enclosed volume whose muscular strength and angulations belie the airy open spaces of the internal living areas. Although it is difficult to deduce from an external viewing, or for that matter an internal viewing, the plan comprises the linear misalignment of two flanking pavilions, both of which are cranked in a dogleg form. Such an arrangement facilitates a succession of internal spaces and external junctions that possess an architectonic rhythm, subtle yet dextrous, utilised to shield the occupants from the sun and heat, especially in the afternoon, whilst maximising the ventilation from the hilltop breezes. K2LD's signature material palette of granite and timber, grandly scaled yet finely detailed, provides a sumptuousness that complements the abiding ambience of spaciousness.

Part of the 92 study models.

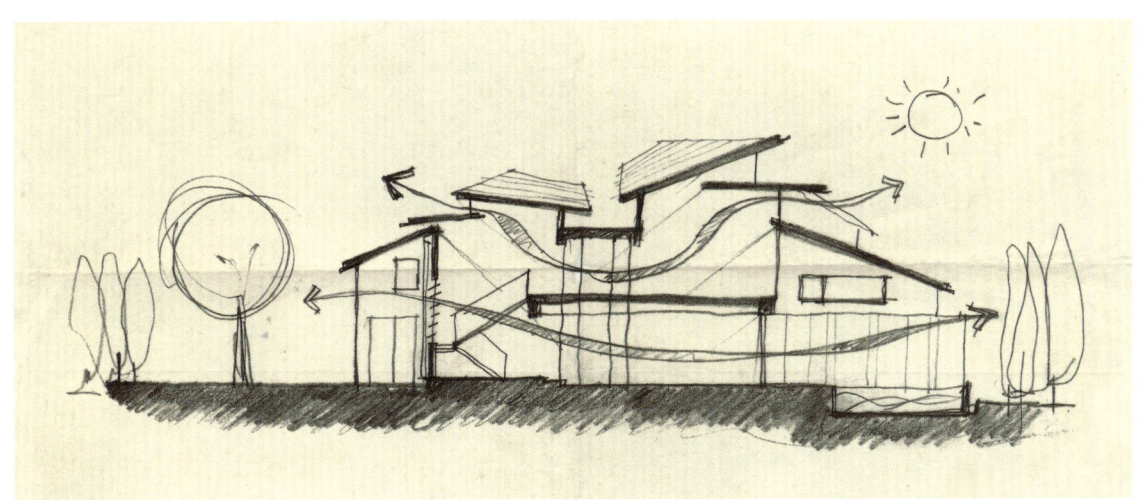

Contrasting lightness of the roof on a heavy concrete base.

Tapering of the roof structure to express the lightness of the Orizuru wing.

"Just think, that man can claim a slice of the sun." – Louis Kahn

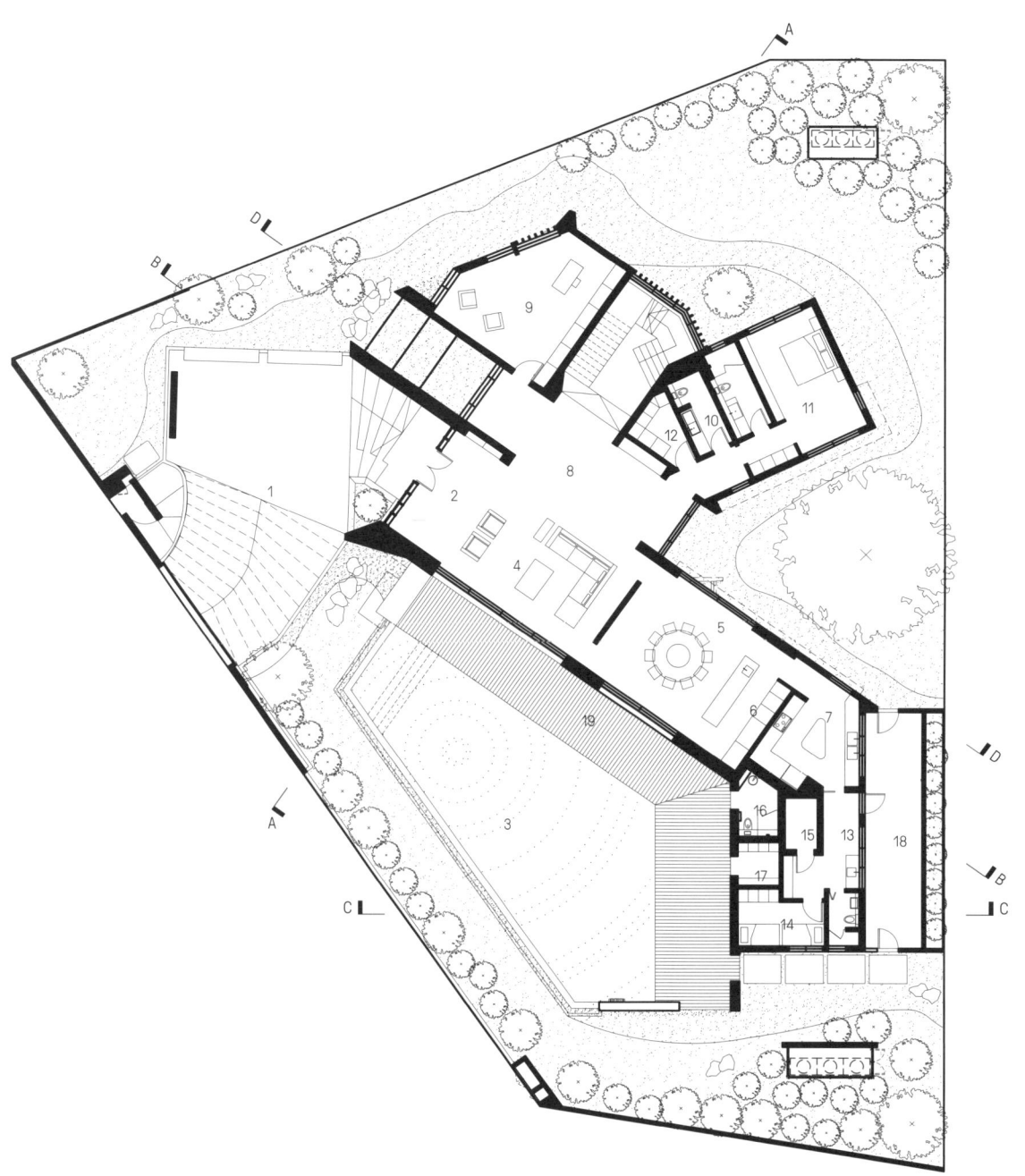

1st storey

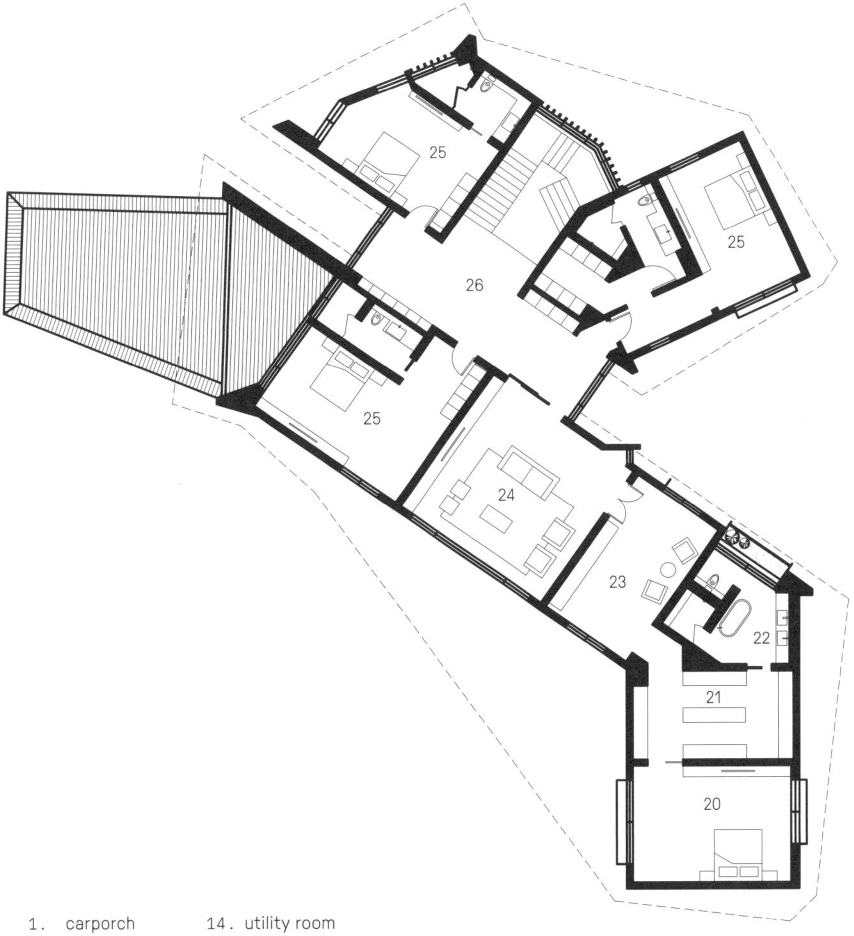

ORIZURU HOUSE — K2LD ARCHITECTS — PLOT 05

1. carporch
2. foyer
3. pool
4. living room
5. dining room
6. dry kitchen
7. wet kitchen
8. passageway
9. study room
10. powder room
11. guest room
12. store
13. laundry
14. utility room
15. hs
16. changing room
17. outdoor store
18. yard
19. outdoor deck
20. master bedroom
21. master bedroom wardrobe
22. master bath
23. master bedroom lounge
24. family room
25. bedroom
26. passage way

2nd storey

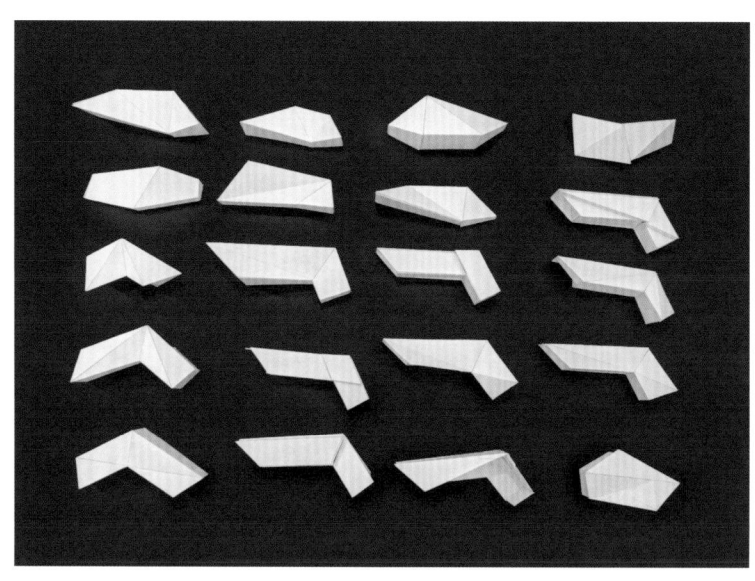

Aerial view that shows the relationship between the Orizuru House and the Old Dalvey House.

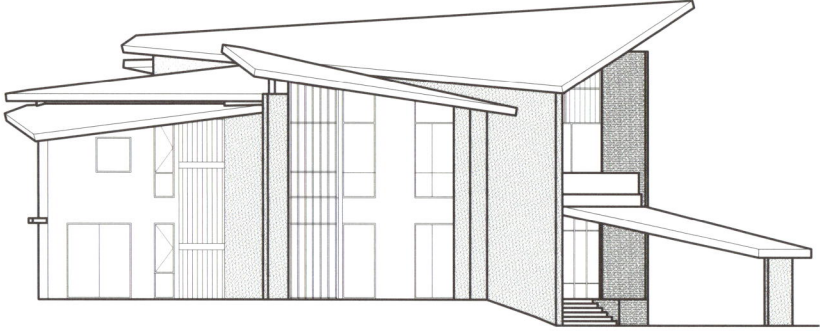

Elevation east

Overlapping roof forms mimic Japanese orizuru origami.

View of the pool from the master bedroom. Large roof overhang provides shade to the pool deck.

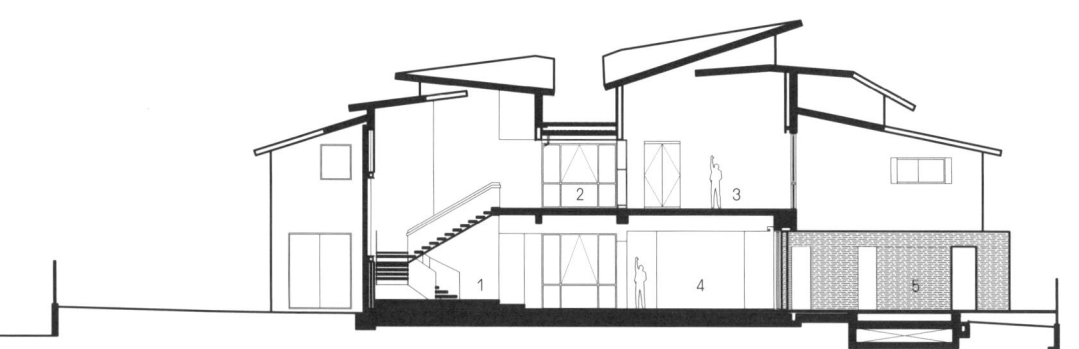

Cross section A through staircase and family room at second storey

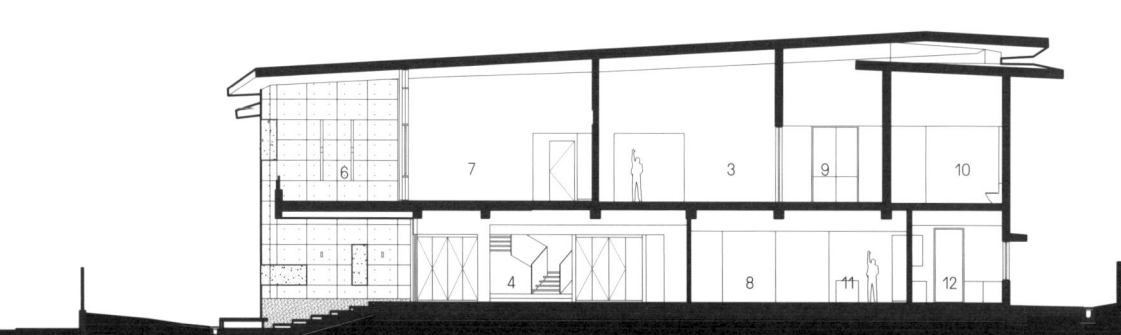

Long section B through living and dining room

1. staircase
2. corridor
3. family room
4. living room
5. outdoor area
6. balcony
7. bedroom
8. dining room
9. master study room
10. master bathroom
11. dry kitchen
12. wet kitchen
13. master bedroom
14. outdoor store room
15. back of house

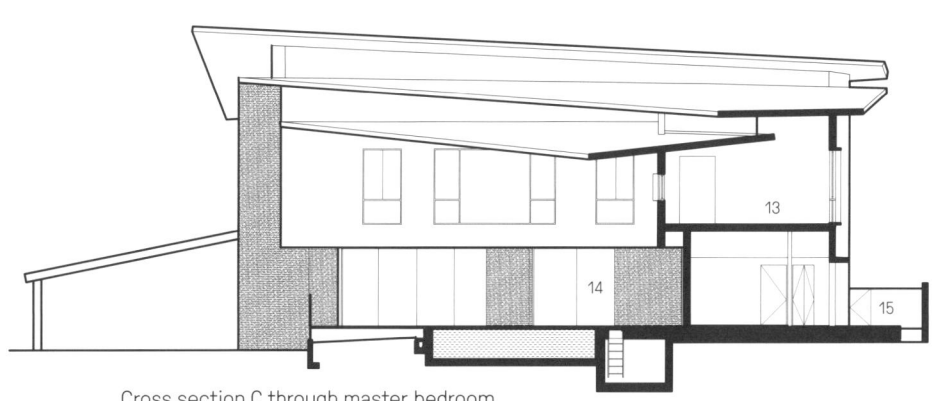

Cross section C through master bedroom

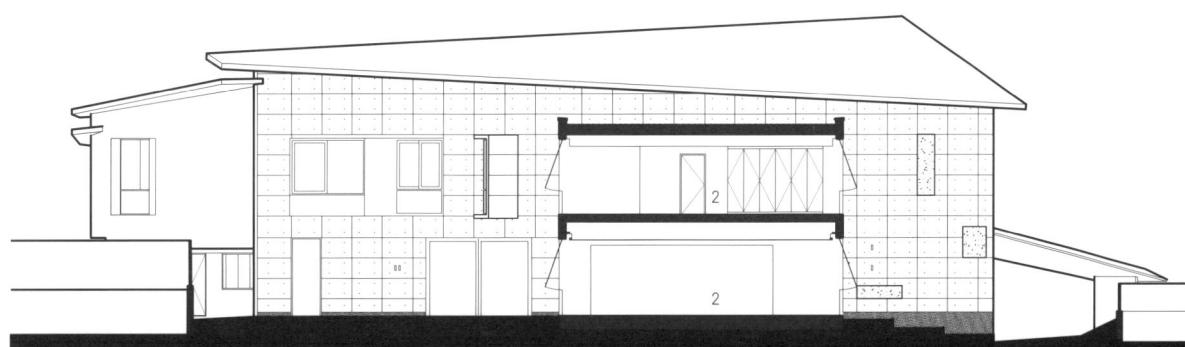

Long section D through connecting volume

Soaring roof form at the front creates a dramatic entry effect, catching a sliver of light in the late afternoon.

Main entrance door detail, cast-in light slot in car porch concrete wall.

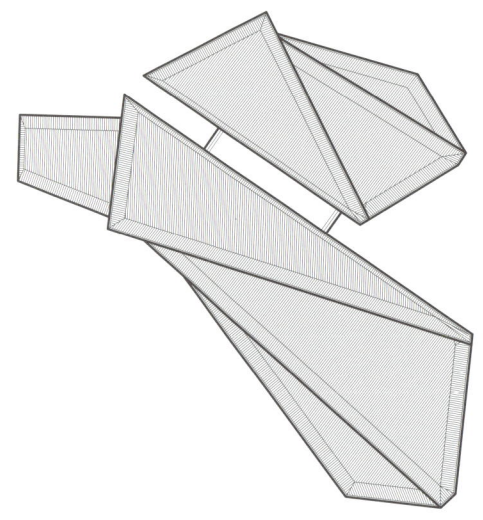

Detail of roof eave.

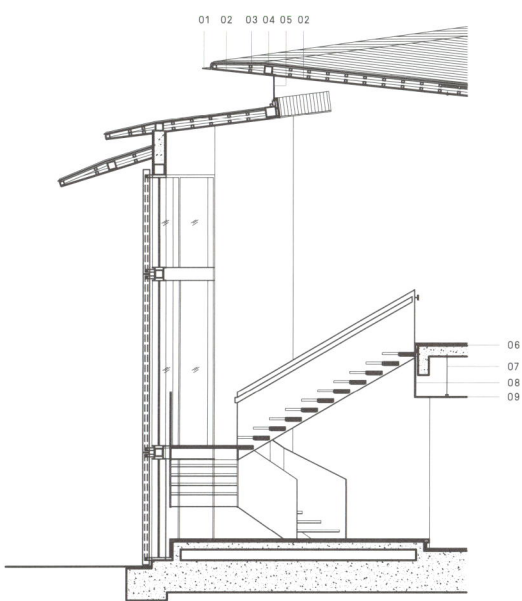

Roof Detail
01. 150 x 50 mm. steel L-angle hot dipped galvanised-steel bar facal in mio paint finish
02. Teak-timber plank
03. 0.7 mm. falzonal aluminium with 25 mm
04. Steel beam
05. Laminated glass, 8 mm. (4+4 thick)
06. Oak engineering timber floor
07. Suspension cable
08. Oxidised-metal sheet, 20mm. THK
09. Ceiling board

Detail of overlapping roofs which let light into the space.

Staircase Detail

01. Steel plate, 20mm. THK
02. Solid timber handrail
03. Solid teak-timber flooring with ply-wood backing
04. Steel plate, 5mm. THK
05. Solid timber to underside of the steps. 20mm. THK chamfered at the edge.
06. 40x200mm, teak solid timber wood
07. 60x10mm, THK metal plate
08. 50x300mm, 5mm THK hot deep galvanised-metal c-profile
09. 200x200mm, RHS hot deep galvanised-steel
10. Laminated glass, 8mm (4+4 thick)

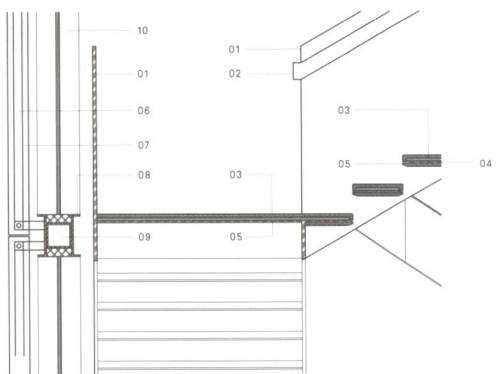
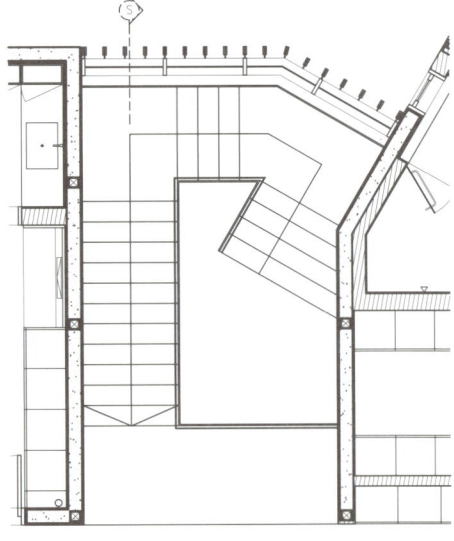

Dramatic staircase geometry.

Detail of staircase handrail.

View of stairs from below catching a glimpse of the overlapping roof.
Lightness of stairs formed by 12mm galvanised-steel plates.

Courtyard spaces receeding to address the Old Dalvey House.

Pebbled edge takes care of the rainwater from the roof eave.

Courtyard looking at the Old Dalvey House by ipli.

ORIZURU HOUSE   K2LD ARCHITECTS   PLOT 05

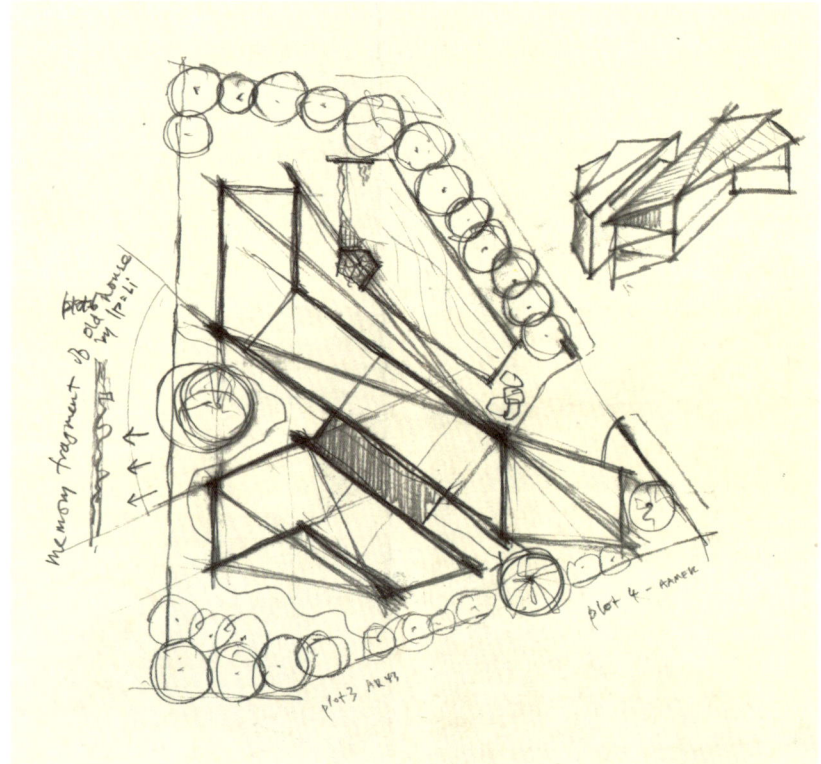

Dramatic soaring roof creates a double volume spatial experience at the outdoor deck. Timber rafter from the Old Dalvey House are reused on the second storey window fenestration to evoke memory of the old house.

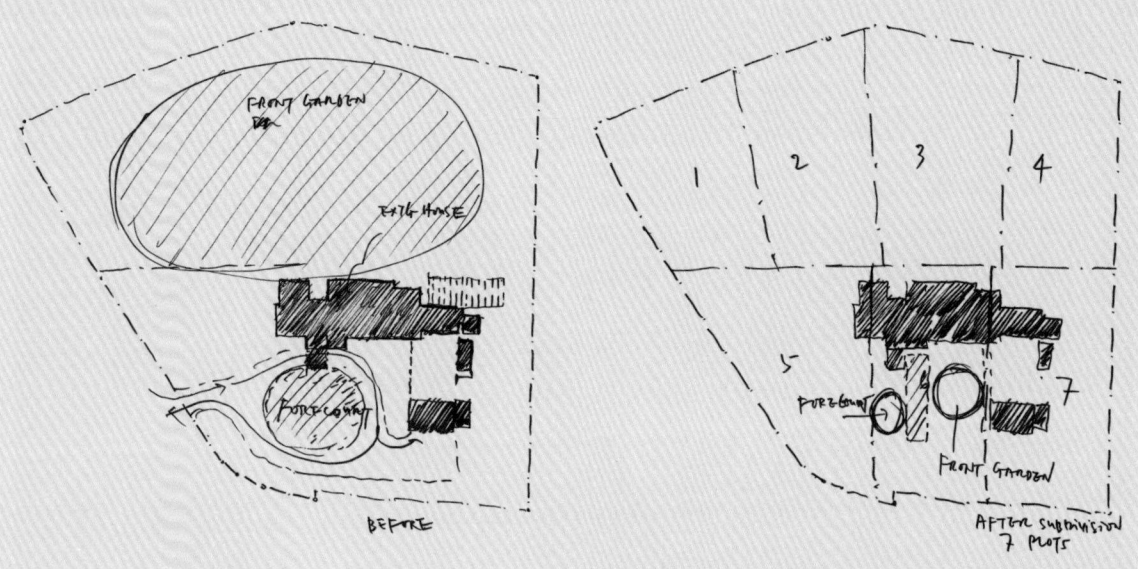
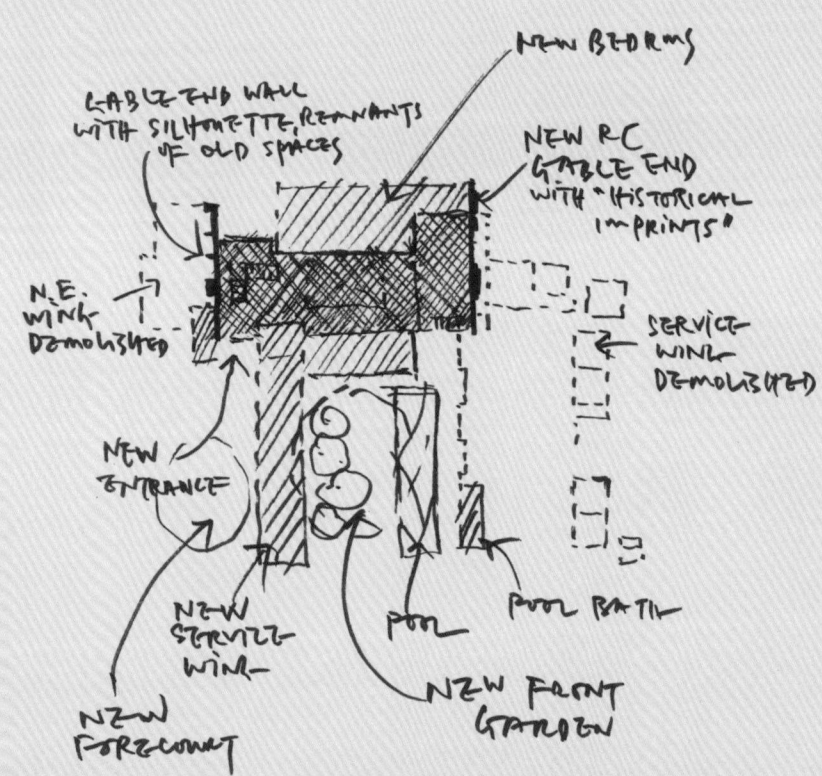

OLD DALVEY

IPLI ARCHITECTS

06

The most intriguing, and possibly the most challenging piece of architecture was undertaken by ipli Architects, who were commissioned to restore and adapt the existing 1950s villa at the centre of the site as the Old Dalvey house. The notion of treating a relatively unremarkable suburban house as an object of veneration was perhaps rather off beat, but ipli have staked an intellectual claim to such an approach, one that is both worthy and idiosyncratic. As it transpired, the resultant architecture was surprisingly compelling, and one is tempted to believe that idiosyncrasy won out, although the unexpectedness of the forms and elevations would not have been possible without the bedrock of the humble bungalow proportions. The original house ran north-south, and due to the nature of the masterplan sub-division, both ends had to be 'lopped off', which allowed the architects to convert the gabled short elevations into structurally revealing sections with a quasi-brutalist expression. The shorter north-south span was then co-opted to form an elongated U plan, which was aligned east-west, and the volumes (and many of the existing 1950s features) of the existing villa were retained for the living and sleeping areas, whilst the new northern wing was used as a services and cooking block, and its southern counterpart for poolside amenities. Built from red bricks in a deliberately rough manner, the walls of these two extrusions have a rather exotic appearance, reminiscent of hot and dry India, and their tactile demeanour was amplified by the juxtaposition of exposed granite-rubble foundations and waffle-slab canopies spluttered with sprayed cement.

Front and rear of the existing house.   Textures, patterns and colours, of the existing house.

Demolition of the existing North-east wing, revealing new gable and wall.

North-west view of the house, with new service wing and pool bath in bricks.

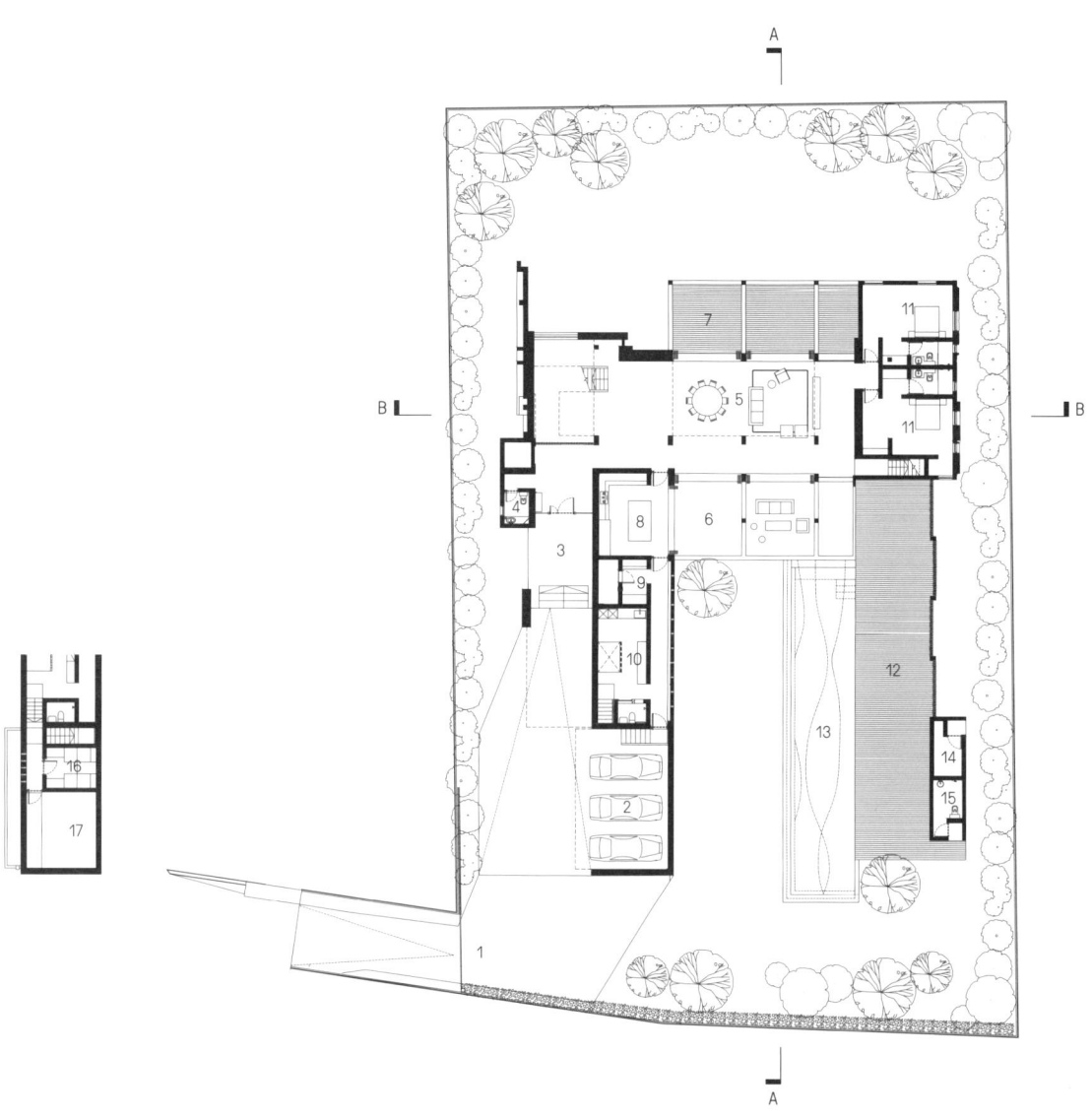

1st storey

1. front gate
2. garage
3. entrance foyer
4. powder room
5. living dining
6. front patio
7. rear patio
8. kitchen
9. store and pantry
10. laundry
11. guest bedroom
12. pool deck
13. swimming pool
14. store
15. pool bath
16. maid room
17. store

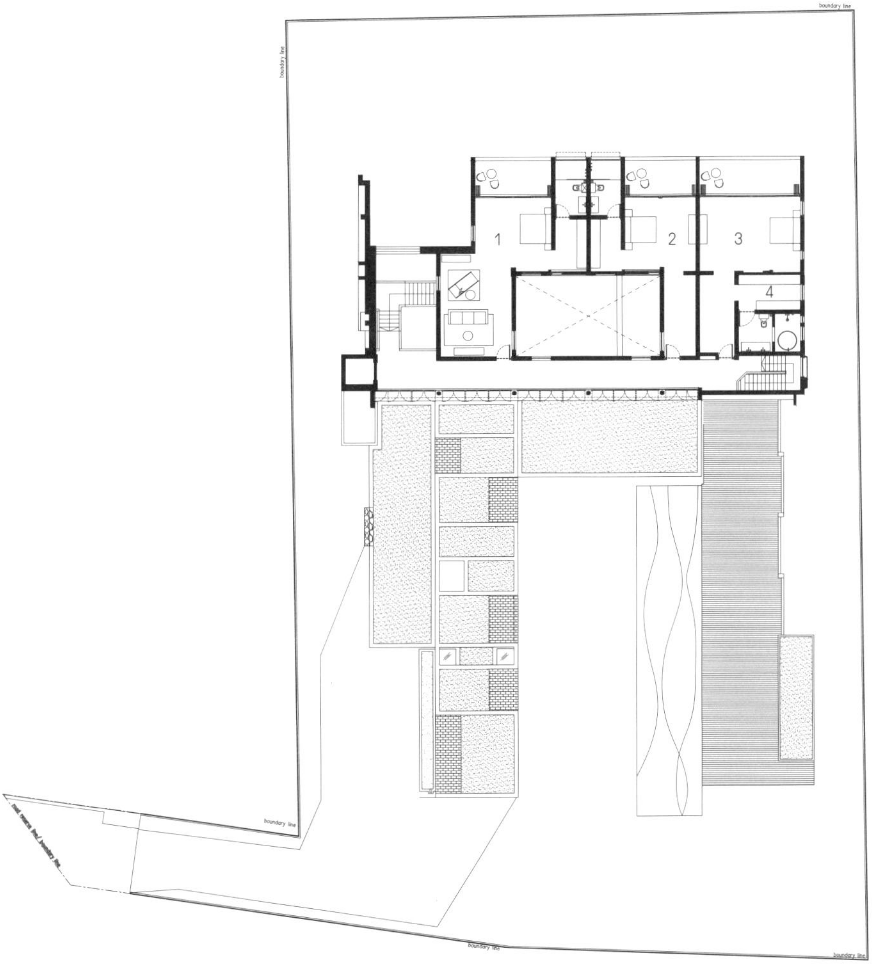

1. bedroom 1
2. bedroom 2
3. master bedroom
4. master bath and wardrobe

2nd storey

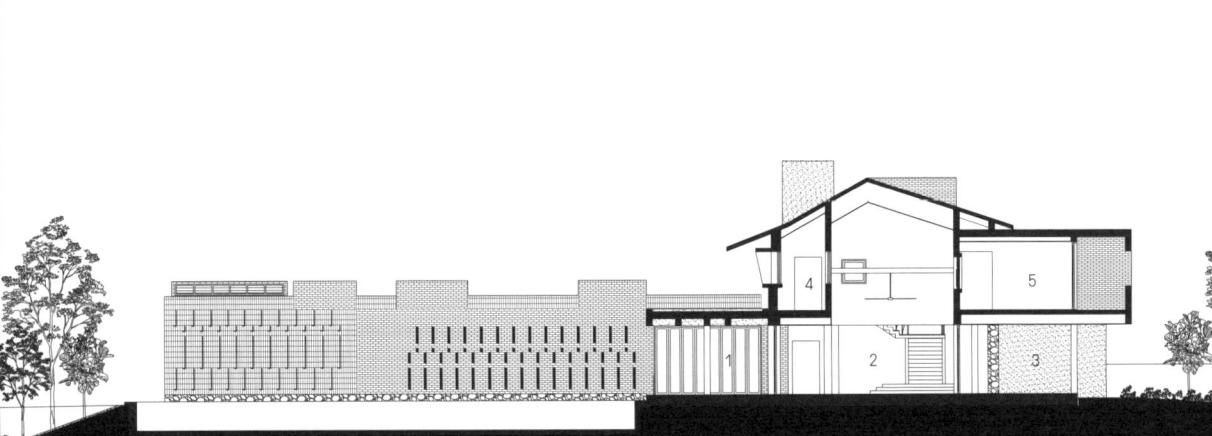

162 – 163　　OLD DALVEY　　　　　IPLI ARCHITECTS　　　　　PLOT 06

Section B

South-east view, with new bedroom extension in bricks over existing terrace.

North-east gable end wall, revealing the silhouette of the original spaces before demolition.

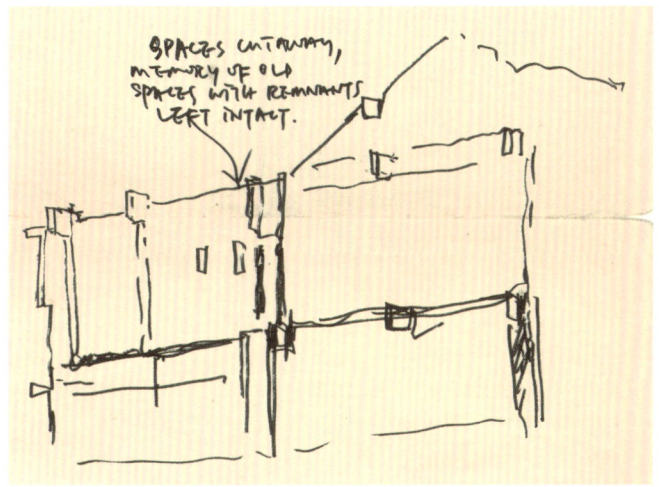

North-east gable end wall.

House entrance with new RC coffered roof supported by existing granite rubble wall.

Front patio.

View from front patio looking at the pool and vegetation beyond.

Side entrance from garage.

New service wing in brick.

New pool bath adjoining existing intricate brick-wall screen.

Entrance screen made from existing window grilles in front of existing stair.

Double volume over living and dining.

Concrete imprints of existing doors and windows viewed from void and from bedroom.

EXTG WALL AS FORMWORK
CONCRETE POURED IN NEW FORMWORK
AFTER FORMWORK REMOVED
NEW RC GABLE END WALL WITH IMPRINTS OF OLD FACADE

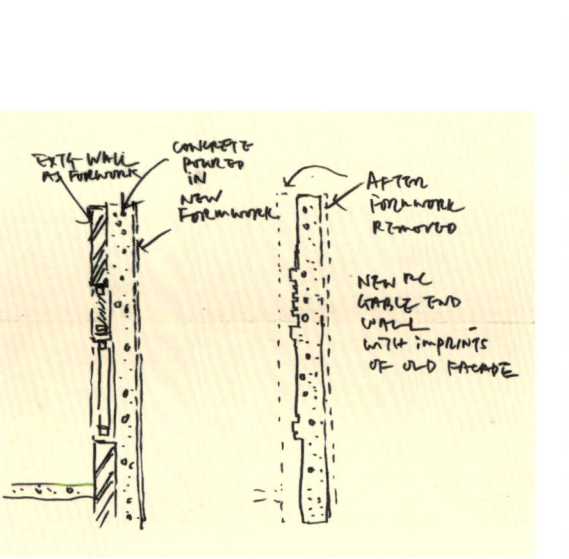

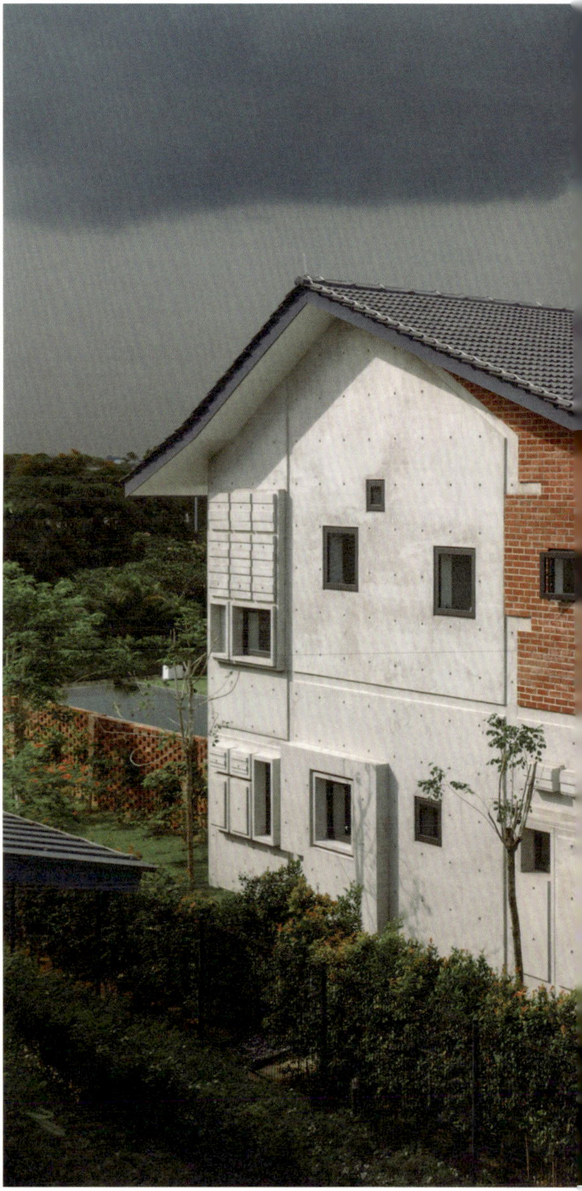

South-west gable end wall, with imprints of existing door and windows adjoining new bedroom extension in bricks.

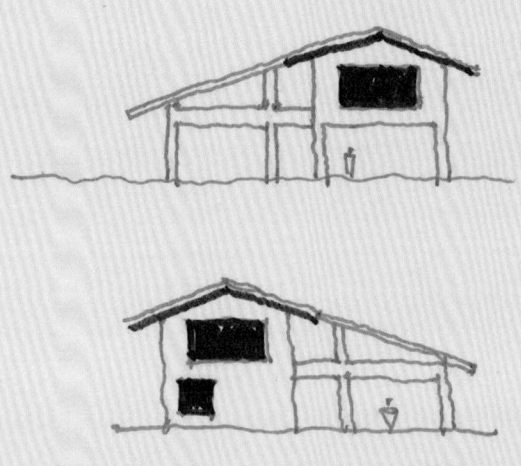
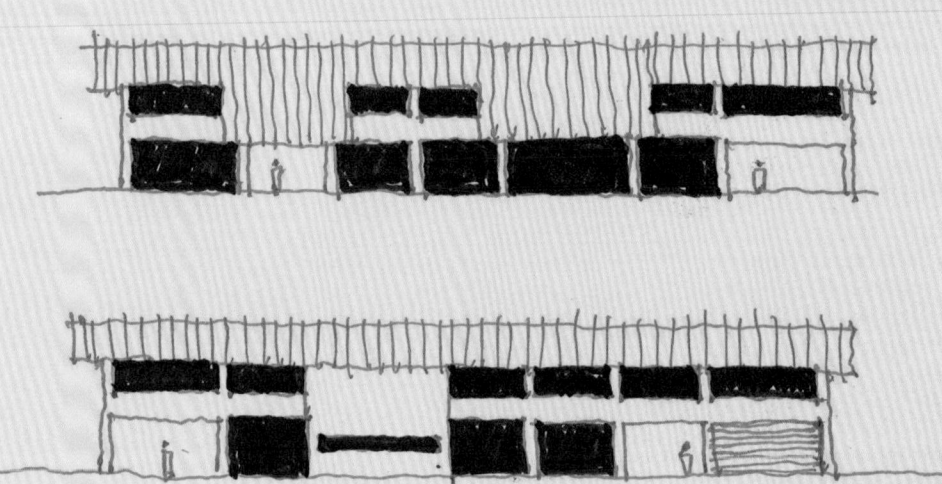

PROJECT	ARCHITECT	PLOT
# LONG HOUSE	## CSYA ARCHITECTS	07

The remaining plot was tucked away on the southern boundary of the Dalvey site, and like the Old Dalvey house, the Long House by CSYA Architects is not visible from the street and was accessed by a driveway from the cul-de-sac. The slender rectangular plot was further secluded, and shaded, by an imposing row of trees in the grounds of Frank Brewer's stately arts and crafts bungalow. Sonny Chan, founder of CSYA and a long-revered local architect, has had an abiding interest in the Black and White houses built a century earlier, and he applied those principles to this house in a manner that was aesthetically abstract but functionally pure. Built from off-form concrete with a metal pitched roof, a unified and permeable linear volume is aligned beneath the row of spreading trees so that natural ventilation can flow through the interiors in a variety of directions. The graciously proportioned scale of the Black and White houses is most immediately apparent in the landscaped enclosures, which adjoin an elongated swimming pool passing beneath one of the two living areas that protrude from the axial main volume. The interior space of the western protrusion forms a wonderful airy and light-filled double volume Formal Living, overlooked by a mezzanine enlivened by a constantly shifting strip of sunlight that shines through a slit at the apex of the roof.

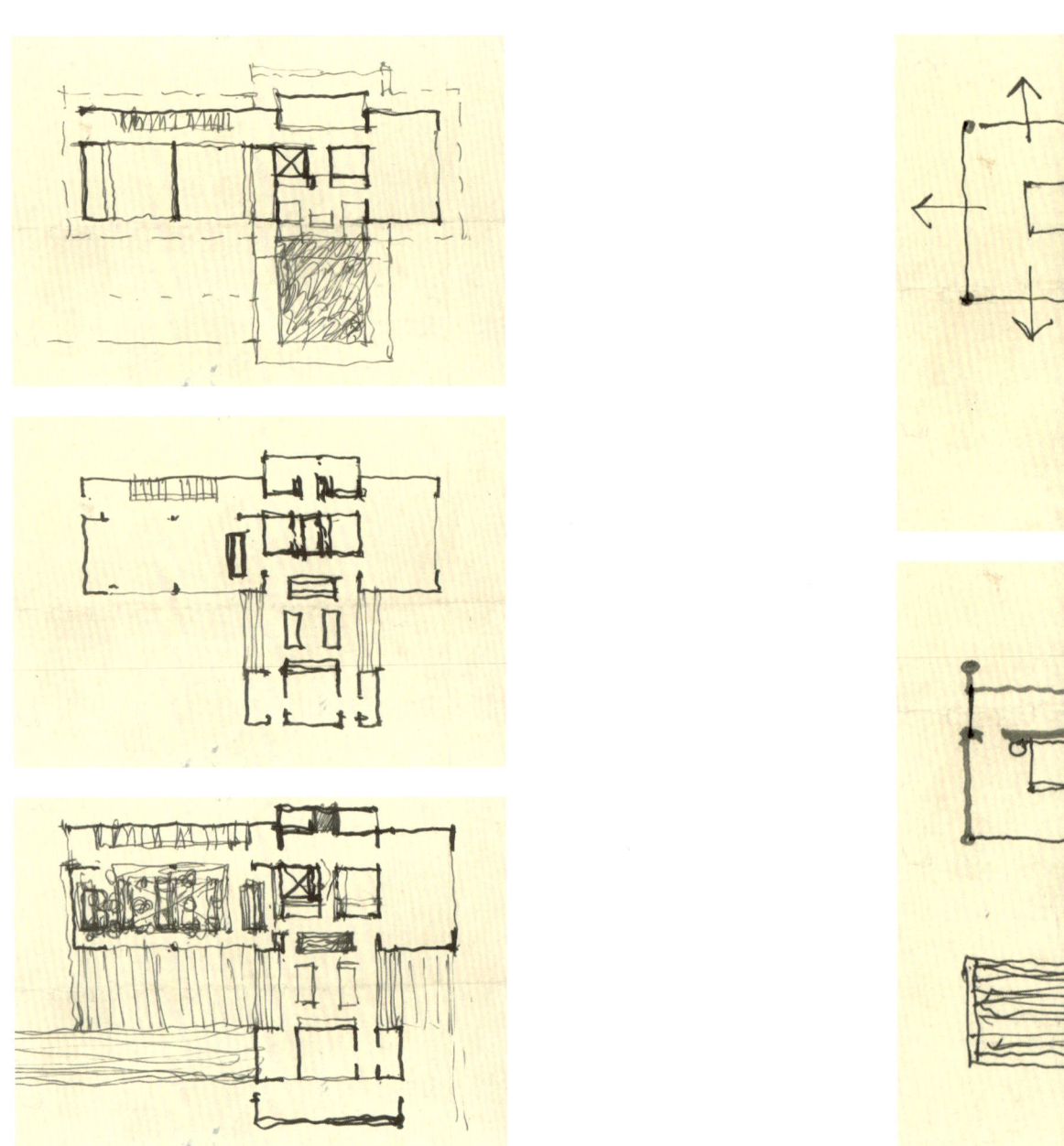

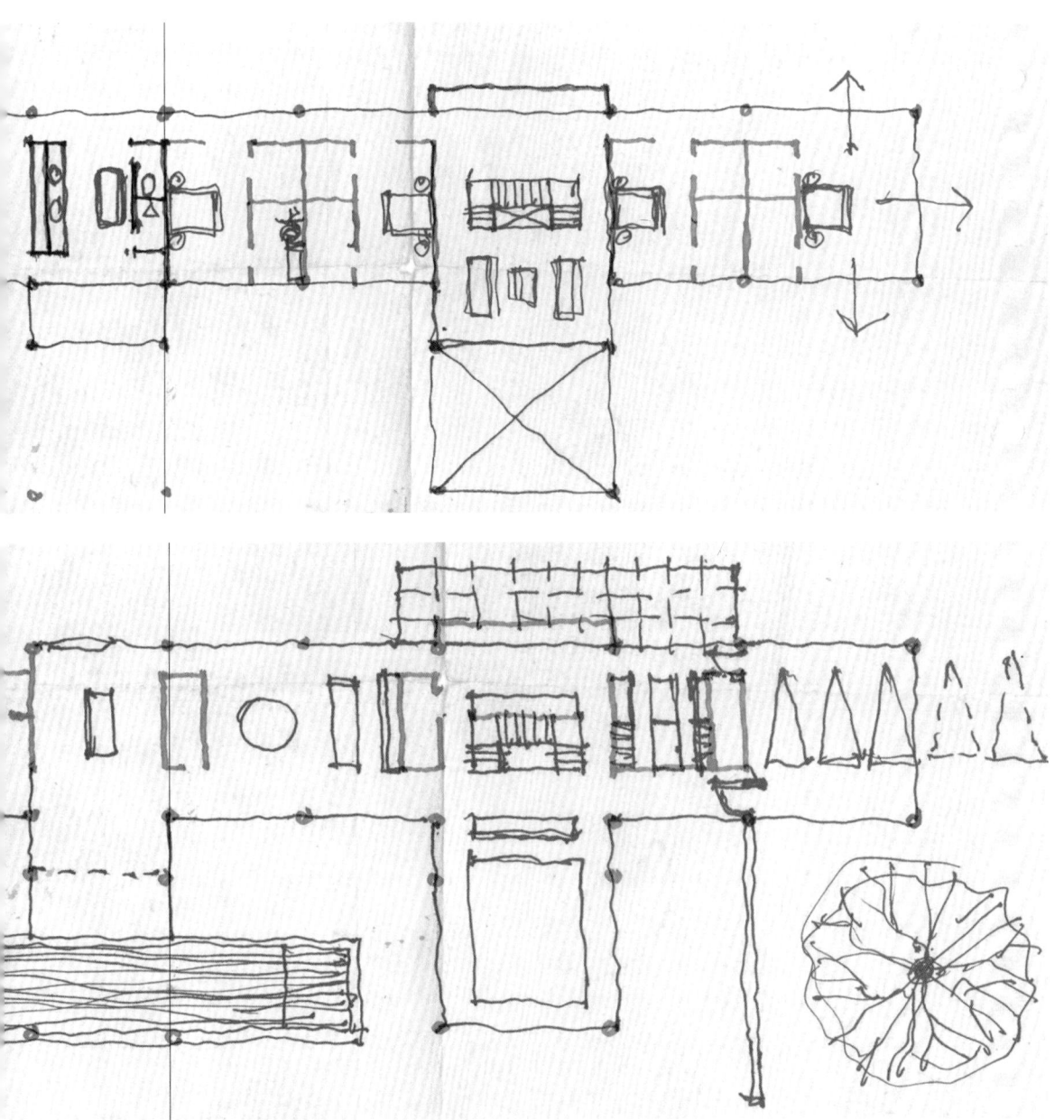

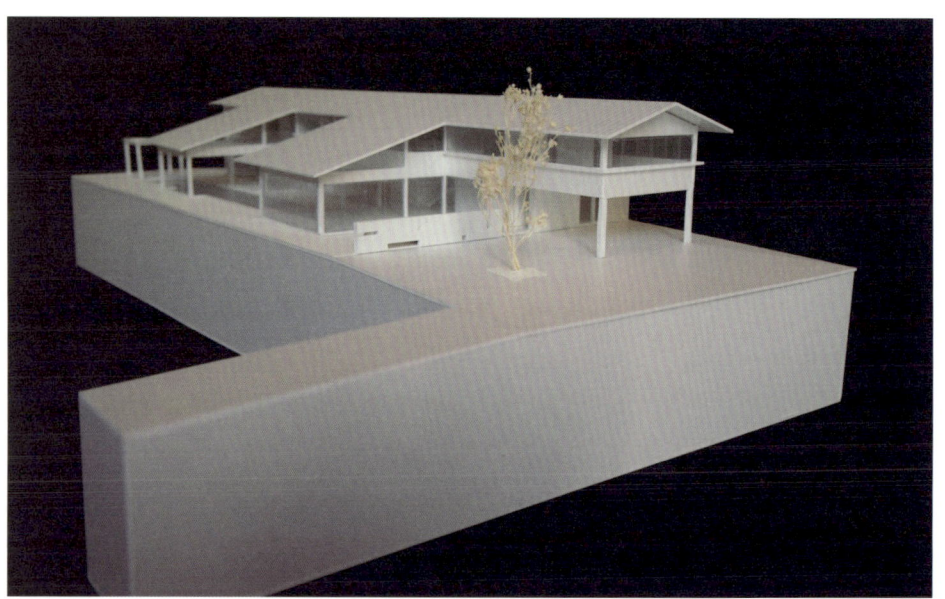

Massing model of proposed development.

The house is set against a backdrop of lush greenery along its longitudinal rear boundary affording natural screening for privacy.

The house reinforces the longitudinal axis by extending across the length of its site.

A mono-pitched roof bridges across the pool to echo the formal living beyond.

Juxtaposition of spaces beneath the mono-pitched roofs is showcased in reverse viewing from the formal living.

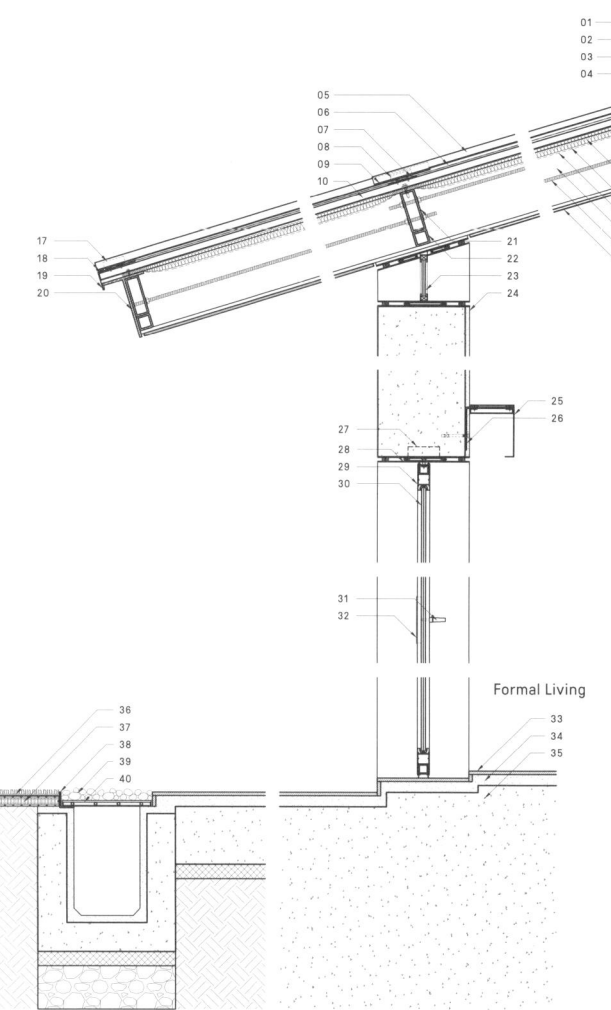

Construction detail

Roof Construction
01. Bent clear acrylic ridge
02. Steel plate
03. Stainless-steel ridge fastening
04. Structural silicone
05. Standing-seam steel-roof cladding
06. Self-adhesive bitumen felt
07. Steel flashing
08. Clip fastening
09. Sealant
10. Steel-roof substrate
11. Thermal insulation
12. Double-sided aluminium foil
13. Safety roof mesh
14. Steel-roof structure
15. Anti-sag rod
16. Ceiling finishes
17. Clip fastening
18. Sealant
19. Steel eave flashing
20. Steel plate
21. Rectangle hollow section
22. Square hollow section

Wall Construction
23. Laminated clear fixed glass in aluminium frame
24. Fair-faced reinforced-concrete beam with plaster and paint finish to interior
25. Aluminium-clad pelmet
26. Concealed steel L-angle
27. Concealed overhead heavy-duty door pivot
28. Aluminium sub-frame
29. Aluminium pivot-door inner frame
30. Laminated clear glass
31. Lever handle with lock
32. Recessed pull handle

Floor Construction
33. Floor finish
34. Cement screed
35. Reinforced-concrete raft foundation floor slab
36. Artificial turf
37. Drainage cell
38. Galvanised-steel L-angle
39. Loose pebbles
40. Drainage grating

A slit of skylight along the ridge line illuminates the family room dramatically.

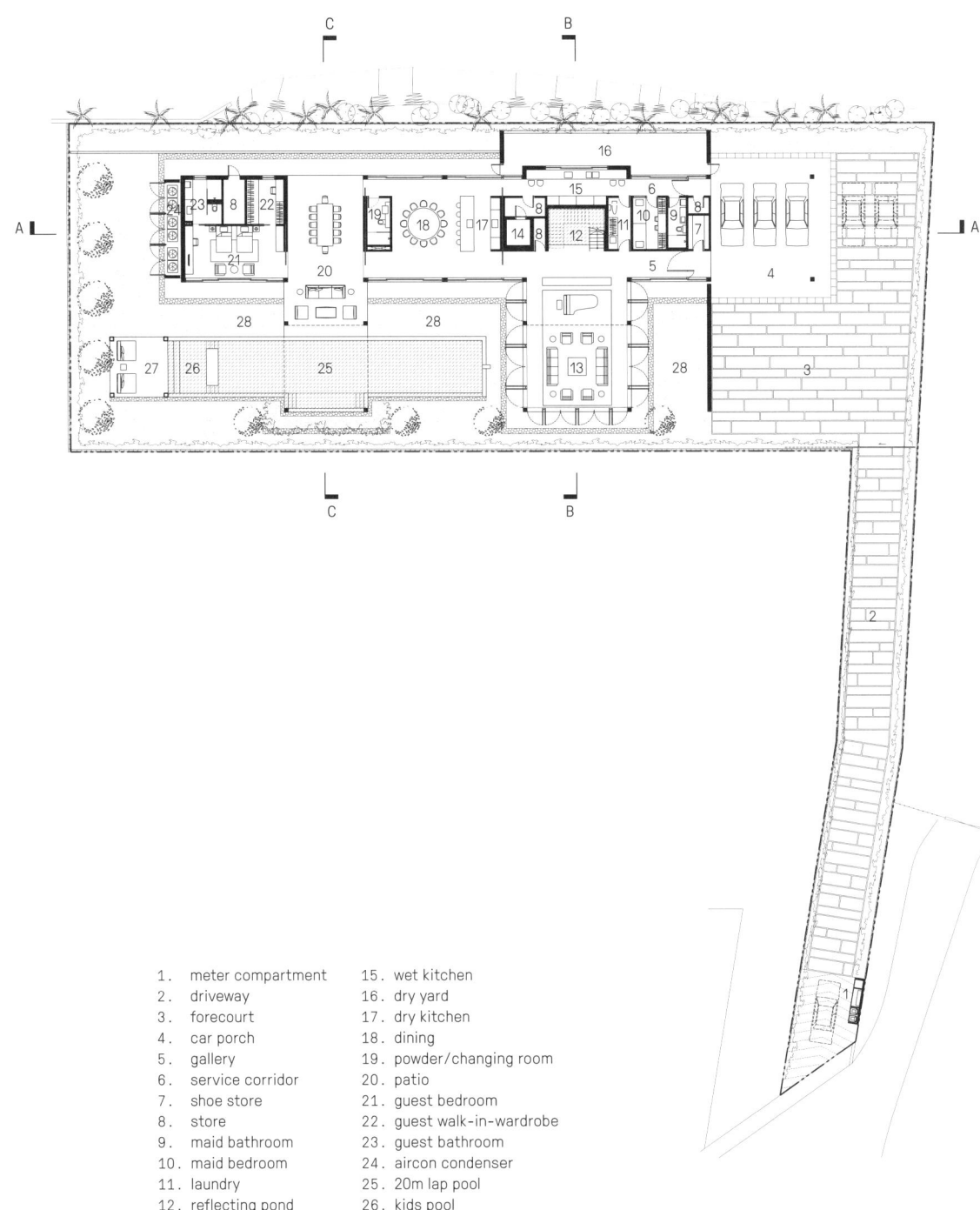

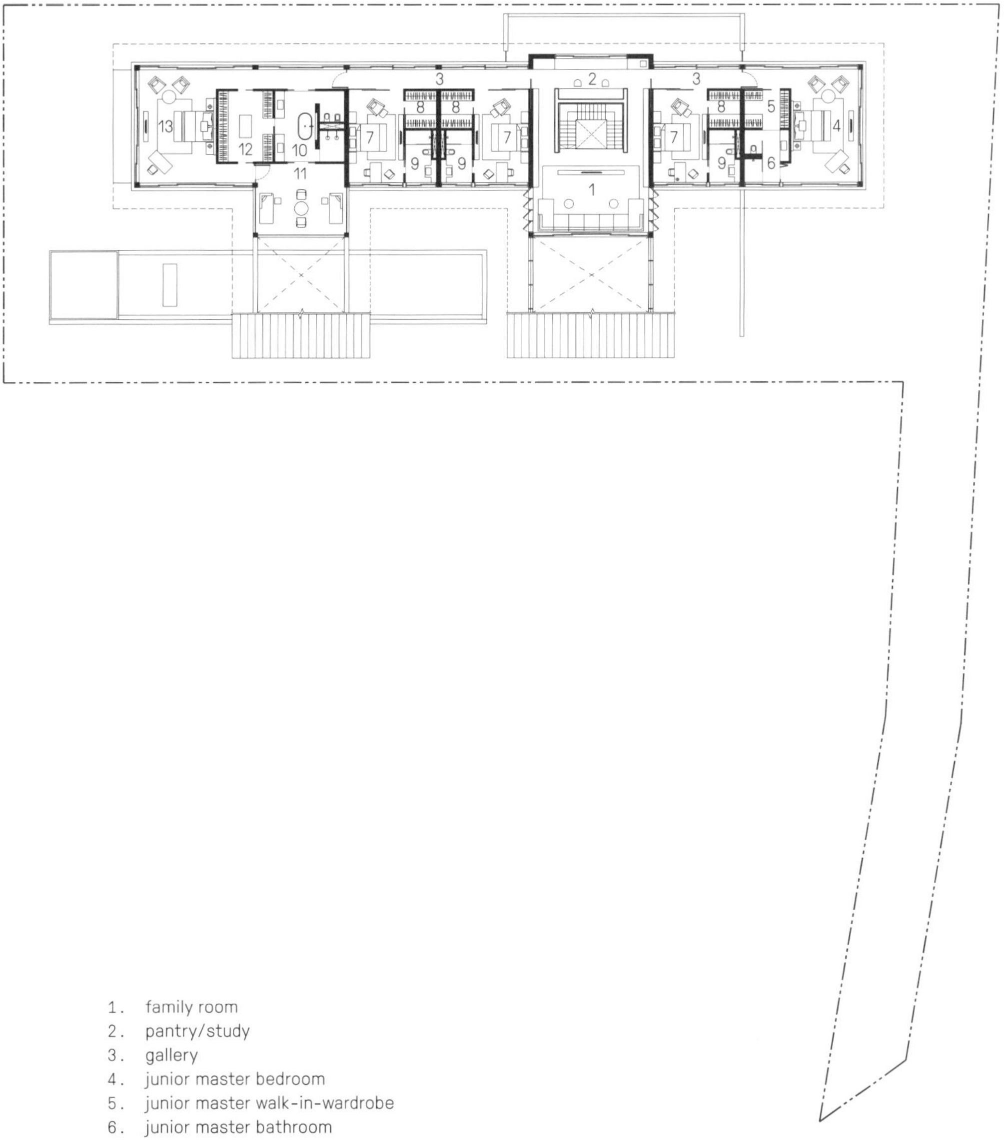

LONG HOUSE — CSYA ARCHITECTS — PLOT 07

1. family room
2. pantry/study
3. gallery
4. junior master bedroom
5. junior master walk-in-wardrobe
6. junior master bathroom
7. typical bedroom
8. typical walk-in-wardrobe
9. typical bathroom
10. master bathroom
11. master balcony
12. master walk-in-wardrobe
13. master bedroom

2nd storey

0 1   10m

Choice of timber in the ceiling is reflected onto the timber-clad staircase adjoining family room and formal living below.

194 – 195 LONG HOUSE CSYA ARCHITECTS PLOT 07

Front elevation

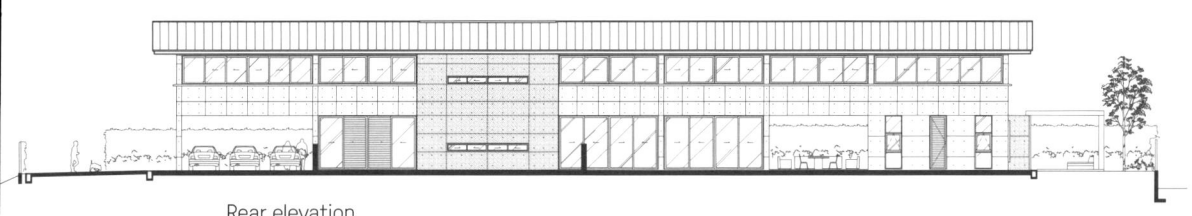

Rear elevation

Longitudinal section A

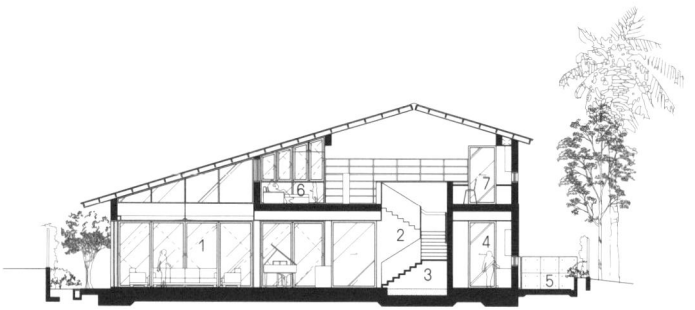

Section B through formal and family room

1. formal living
2. staircase
3. reflecting pond
4. wet kitchen
5. dry yard
6. family room
7. pantry/study

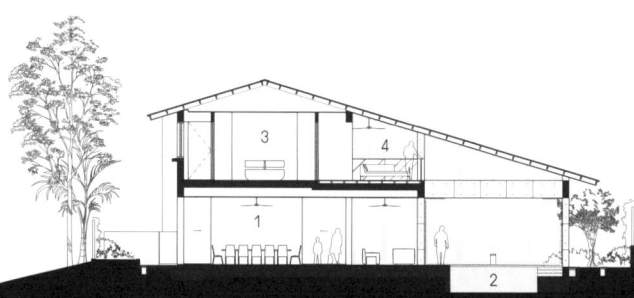

Section C through patio and master balcony

1. patio
2. lap pool

Roof Construction
01. Steel-ridge capping
02. End closure
03. Clip fastening
04. Substrate ridge flashing
05. Standing-seam steel-roof cladding
06. Self-adhesive bitumen felt
07. Steel-roof substrate
08. Thermal insulation
09. Double-sided aluminium foil
10. Safety roof mesh
11. Clip fastening
12. Steel flashing
13. Sealant
14. Steel-roof structure
15. Anti-sag rod
16. Rectangle hollow section
17. Square hollow section
18. Ceiling finishes

Wall Construction
19. Stainless-steel U-channel
20. Laminated clear glass
21. Sealant
22. Backer rod
23. Aluminium U-channel

Floor Construction
24. Floor finishes
25. Square hollow section
26. Rectangle hollow section
27. Steel L-angle
28. Nut and bolt
29. Cement screed
30. Cementitious waterproofing
31. Fairfaced concrete structure
32. Suspension cable
33. Furring channel track
34. Furring channel
35. Ceiling finishes
36. Floor finishes
37. Reinforced-concrete pool structure
38. Underwater light fitting
39. Coping finishes
40. Stainless-steel flat bar
41. Cement screed
42. Waterproofing membrane
43. Wall finishes
44. Artificial turf
45. Drainage cell
46. Stainless-steel L-angle
47. Loose pebbles
48. Drainage grating

Master Balcony

Construction detail

Lap Pool

Patio

Long House and its garden setting as reflected in the evening.

Semi-outdoor spaces including patio and master balcony are extended to meet the lap pool.

THE SEVEN ARCHITECTS

WALLFLOWER ARCHITECTS

Wallflower Architects was founded by Robin Tan and Cecil Chee, bringing together a combined experience of residential developments and commercial projects. Established in 1999, Wallflower Pte Ltd & Wallflower Architecture + Design have undertaken a wide spectrum of work, ranging from commercial and residential projects and have received numerous awards for excellence in design, having been also extensively featured in local and international publications. Wallflower believes that beauty and cleverness are inseparable in excellent design, the value of which enhances the environment in which we work and live and ultimately, enriches the human experience and spirit.

GUZ ARCHITECTS

Guz Architects seeks to produce refreshing architecture that is tranquil, inspired by nature, yet human in scale. Their projects both derive inspiration from, and relate closely to nature. Structure, materials and technology are used to express as seamless a transition as possible between inside and outside. The resulting designs are both responsive and responsible to the site and its occupants, with consideration being given to the integration and preservation of the surrounding natural environment. Their practice makes extensive use of sustainable design technologies, and both passive and active design principles inform all design decisions with the intent to create long lasting, timeless architecture.

AR43 ARCHITECTS

AR43 Architects is an award winning firm established in 2006 by Lim Cheng Kooi. The firm has been characterised as being strongly committed in the pursuits of responsible design. Within a span of 12 years, it has made a profound mark within the design and architectural field. Its philosophy in being responsive to the context of the place, the importance of the clients' needs and solving the issues of the moment has successfully propelled the firm to greater heights, taking on a multitude of building projects.

AAMER ARCHITECTS

Aamer Architects is a boutique architectural firm, since 1994, that views design as finding an ideal solution to a combination of factors including environment, culture, climate, structure & services with an economy of means to arrive at an aesthetic "completeness" – archisculpture. Each project is seen as a work of art, conceived through a thorough appreciation of site, context and brief, and carefully sculpted to pleasantly fit into the site while keeping the client's brief intact. Aamer Taher was trained in Singapore [NUS] and in London [Architectural Association School of Architecture].

K2LD ARCHITECTS

K2LD Architects is an international practice established in Singapore in 1998 and in Melbourne in 2007. Their architectural design philosophy embraces the sense and sensibility of architecture. The senses mould the intricate relationship between time, light and material to allow spatial freedom that is beautiful in its myriad of expressions. Taming these exciting relationships materialises in an architectural experience. The sensibilities of architecture advocate an understanding of the ways the natural beauty of materials can be brought out in construction, enhancing the imaginative appreciation of the way in which materials partake in the design.

ipli ARCHITECTS

After a combined working experience of more than two and a half decades in the architectural profession, Yip Yuen Hong and Lee Ee Lin, the principals of ipli Architects decided to form a practice with a core philosophy and aspirations that would match their own professional and personal ambitions. Passionate about design and architecture, they were torn between giving every project the attention and time they deserved, with the economics of running a business. This was a constant source of frustration for both but they took on the challenge and ipli Architects was formed in 2001.

CSYA ARCHITECTS

CSYA Pte Ltd provides full architectural services including master planning, concept and detailed design, documentation and supervision, in addition to full interior design service, and is active regionally and internationally. Founded in 1993, formerly known as Chan Sau Yan Associates and CSYA Studio Pte Ltd to undertake local and overseas project respectively, the firm is incorporated as CSYA Pte Ltd in 2012. The firm is committed to design innovation and the integration of appropriate technology. It firmly believes that design excellence requires the close and active collaboration of the client supported equally by the skills of the specialist consultants.

The 7 gurus.

PROJECT DATA

TEAM MEMBERS

See Through House by
Wallflower Architects
Robin Tan, Sean Zheng, Shirley Tan,
Carlo Borromeo and Eileen Kok

Sail House by
Guz Architects
Guz Wilkinson and Lee Rong Rong

Tembusu House by
AR43 Architects
Lim Cheng Kooi and Murphy Wong

Gallery House by
Aamer Architects
Aamer Taher, Jasni Ngahtemin,
Evy Sutjahjo and Zixu Loh
(Interior Design by
Fuseproject Pte Ltd)

Orizuru House by
K2LD Architects
Ko Shiou Hee, Charlotte Wong,
Fiorella Amadei and Younha Kim

Old Dalvey by
ipli Architects
Yip Yuen Hong, Tay Yew,
Szeto Yan Mae and Lin Hui Ying

Long House by
CSYA Architects
Chan Sau Yan, Chen Huihua,
Nary Chea and Hashia Hashim

Civil & Structural Engineer
MSE Consultants Pte Ltd - Andrew Teo,
John Lim, Gan Khai Sin, Zayar Minn,
Anistonraj Mariya and Vinsonclero Theonis

Mechanical & Electrical Engineer
LAC Engineers & Associates - Adeline Chua

Quantity Surveyor
WS Surveyorship Pte Ltd

Landscape Work
Greenery Horticultural Pte Ltd

Builder
Daiya Engineering & Construction Pte Ltd

Carpentry
Stema Furniture & Renovation Pte Ltd

CREDITS

CONTRIBUTORS

Erwin Viray is the current professor and head of pillar at the Singapore University of Technology and Design. He was also the Global Excellence Professor at Kyoto Institute of Technology and Head of the Graduate School of Architecture and Design in 2012 for two years. In addition, he holds several professional leadership roles including Chief Communications Officer for the Kyoto Design Lab and a member of the Singapore President's Design Awards jury since 2012 and the chair of the jury since 2013. He is also an award ambassador for the HolcimLafarge Awards in Asia Pacific, a jury chair of archiprix SEA 2012 and 2016, a member of management board the TOTO Gallery MA, an advisory council member for the Barcelona Institute of Architecture. Erwin has been editor of the influential magazine, *a+u (Architecture + Urbanism)* since 1996.

Ko Shiou Hee began his career with Morphosis, then moved on to Kohn Pederson & Fox, followed by IM Pei in the US, before returning to Asia. He then spent two years in Tokyo as a design consultant. In 1993, he decided to return to Singapore and set up K2LD Architects in 2000. He's also the co-author of *No Boundaries – The Lien Villa Collection*. In the article "The Master Planner's Game Theory", Ko explained the practical application of the theory in architectural collaboration.

Patrick Bingham-Hall is an architectural photographer who came to prominence in the 1990s. He is also an architectural writer and editor, and owns Pesaro Publishing, which publishes books on architecture and design.

IMAGE CREDITS

Albert Lim ©:
089 097 103 104 105

APVT Media Productions ©:
004 139 186

David Ewen ©:
012-top

Google Maps 2020 ©:
012-center 027

Jennifer Purple Passport ©:
012-bottom 022

K2LD Architects ©:
016 017 024 025 028 029 141
146-right 147-left
148-right 149 151-right
203 204

Khoogj ©: 177

Patrick Bingham-Hall ©:
042 046 048 049 053 054 055
056 064 068 071 072 076 077
081 088 090 092 093 100 112
114 115 123 124 126 127
134 140 144 145 146-left
147-right 148-left 150
151-left 153 164 166 167
184 188 189 191 194 198 200

Studio Periphery ©:
158 168 169 170 172 173 174
175

Wei Kuan Tay ©:
121 122 128